Best Value Books™

Grammar Grades 9-10

Table of Contents

© Carson Dellosa CD-3745
i
ISBN 0-88724-501-3

About the Book

Grammar Grades 9-10

Prepared by: Kelley Wingate Levy
Written By: Dr. Vicki Gallo Sullivan

This book is just one in our Best Value™ series of reproducible, skill oriented activity books. Each book is developmentally appropriate and contains over 100 pages packed with educationally-sound, classroom-tested activities. Each book also contains skill cards and resource pages with extended activity ideas.

The activities in this book have been developed to help students master the basic skills necessary to succeed in grammar. The activities have been sequenced to help insure successful completion of the assigned tasks, thus building positive self-esteem, as well as the self-confidence students need to meet academic challenges.

The activities may be used by themselves, as supplemental activities, or as enrichment material for a grammar program.

Developed by teachers and tested by students, we never lost sight of the fact that if students don't stay motivated and involved, they will never truly grasp the skills being taught on a cognitive level.

About the author...

Dr. Vicki Gallo Sullivan has spent twenty-plus years in the business/art of educating children. With areas of specialization in reading, curriculum and instruction, and gifted education, she has run the teaching gamut from elementary and secondary to the university level. Her direct experience with children ranges from classroom teacher and Reading Specialist to Chapter 1 Coordinator and Gifted Resource Instructor. She has taught curriculum courses for over a decade at several universities in Louisiana. Dr. Sullivan has also served as an External Assessor in the Louisiana Teacher Assessment Program.

Outside the field of education, Dr. Sullivan works as a travel consultant in a family-owned and run travel agency. Being deeply stricken with wanderlust herself, she often shares her enthusiasm for both foreign and domestic destinations. Much of the subject matter in this book is a direct result of her travels.

Ready-to-Use Ideas and Activities

The activities in this book will help children master the basic skills necessary to become competent learners. Remember as you read through the activities listed below and as you go through this book, that all children learn at their own rates. Although repetition is important, it is critical that we never lose sight of the fact that it is equally important to build children's self-esteem and self-confidence if we want them to become successful learners.

Skill card ideas

The back of this book has removable skill cards that will be helpful for basic skill and enrichment activities. Pull the skill cards out and cut them apart (if you have access to a paper cutter, use that). Following are several ideas for use of the skill cards.

Have students write sentences that summarize a story or lesson. Use the **parts of speech cards (#1-8)** to sort the words used in the sentences.

Take out the **verb tense cards (#9-14)** and twenty-five **sentence skill cards (#15-39).**

1. Have students place each verb card in the correct tense category. As a group, check the verbs in each category.

2. Shuffle the verb tense cards and place face up on the table. Shuffle the sentence cards and place face up next to the verb tense cards. The student should number a piece of paper from one to 25. Each student takes one verb tense and one sentence card from the top of the deck. The task is to change the sentence so the verb will match the verb tense card. Write the new sentence on the paper. Continue until all the sentences have been rewritten.

3. Have students write all eight verb tenses (**#9-14**) using verbs you supply. (example: marry, graduate, tell, travel, finish)

4. Have students use the verb tense cards to help them find and identify all six tenses in newspaper or magazine articles.

Ready-to-Use Ideas and Activities

Select the **subject and predicate skill cards (#40-54)**.

1. Have students create sentences that demonstrate each type of subject and predicate combination on the flash cards.

2. Have students find each type of subject and predicate combination in magazine or newspaper articles. Highlight or cut out the sentences and place them under the correct card.

3. Have students write five to ten simple subject and simple predicate sentences. Use the subject and predicate flash cards to expand the sentence as the flashcard dictates. For example:
   simple sentence: Students reviewed.
   flashcard **#48:** Students reviewed thoroughly for the exam.
   flashcard **#49:** The serious students reviewed.
   flashcard **#50:** Students and teachers reviewed.
   flashcard **#51:** The serious students reviewed thoroughly for the exam.
   flashcard **#52**: Students reviewed thoroughly for the exam and practiced for a long time.
   flashcard **#53:** Students and teachers reviewed and practiced.
   flashcard **#54:** The serious students and their worried teachers reviewed thoroughly for the exam and practiced for a long time.

Select the **sentence pattern cards (#55-59)** and the **sentence cards (#70-79)**.

1. Match the sentences with the correct pattern.

2. Have students write their own sentences that match the five sentence patterns.

3. Shuffle the sentence pattern cards and place upside-down on the table. Repeat with the sentence cards. Students take turns selecting a pattern card and drawing sentences until they find a match.

Ready-to-Use Ideas and Activities

Select the **diagraming cards (#60-66)** and the **sentence cards (#70-79)**.

1. Have the students make two diagrams for each of the sentence cards. One will be the basic sentence pattern parts and the other will contain all modifiers (adjectives, adverbs, and prepositional phrases).

2. Have the students write two original sentences that fit in each basic diagram category. Diagram each.

3. Using the student sentences constructed in the above activity (2), have them add modifiers and construct a second sentence diagram that includes the modifiers.

Select the **clause cards (#82-83)** and the clauses **(#84-96)** .

1. Individually or in pairs, have the students separate each clause into the "dependent" or "independent" stack. Check the work as a group.

2. Have the students rewrite the clauses (**#84-96**). For the independent clauses, have them expand the sentence by adding a dependent clause. Have the students add an independent clause to the dependent clauses to create a complete sentence.

3. Pair the students. They are to each write five independent clauses and exchange papers. The partners add a dependent clause to each sentence. This can also be reversed, beginning with dependent clauses.

4. Have the students find ten examples of dependent clauses in newspapers, magazines, and catalogs. Highlight the sentence and underline the dependent clause.

5. Cut dependent clauses from newspapers, magazines, and catalogs. Have students write a new independent clause for each dependent clause.

Concrete and Abstract

A **concrete noun** names an object which can be perceived by the senses.
An **abstract noun** names a quality, characteristic, or an idea.

Examples: Concrete: dress, fire, table, noise
　　　　　 Abstract: democracy, hatred, beauty, happiness

Underline the concrete nouns and circle the abstract nouns in each sentence.

1. His depression continued long after the death of his wife.

2. The beggar felt hunger on a daily basis.

3. The people witnessed the collision on their way to church.

4. The computer was left on by my sister.

5. Yesterday was rainy and overcast.

6. Will you graduate before the end of this century?

7. The magazine rack was overstuffed.

8. The dictionary on the desk is unabridged.

9. The crystal goblet fell and shattered.

10. The door was locked, and I had forgotten the key.

11. The people did not choose the harsh dictatorship.

12. The paper was covered with finger paint.

13. The woman brought the ticket to her employer.

14. There is an anti-war theme to the novel.

15. The strength of the storm was impressive.

Collective Nouns

A **collective noun** names a group as if it were one individual. The collective noun uses a singular verb when the group is referred to as a unit. It uses a plural verb when the individuals in the group are regarded separately.

Examples: The vote of the committee was unanimous. (singular)
                         The committee have continued to argue among themselves.   (plural)

Underline the collective noun. In the blank write S if it is used as a singular noun or P if it is plural.

_____ 1. The jury could not agree on a verdict in the case.

_____ 2. The jury has its own reserved parking spaces.

_____ 3. The new family next door has a West Highland White Terrier.

_____ 4. The family were seated around the television.

_____ 5. The crew has taken a vote and decided on a mutiny.

_____ 6. The crew are coming on board to prepare their stations for the cruise.

_____ 7. The majority has elected an independent candidate for president.

_____ 8. The majority of the seniors are interested in a cruise for their class trip.

_____ 9. The Jefferson High team won the division.

_____ 10. After graduation, the team are going their separate ways.

Write a sentence using the collective noun "class" in the singular form. Write a second sentence using "class" as a plural collective noun.

1. _____

2. _____

Plural Compound Nouns

Compound nouns form their plurals by adding *-s* to the most important word in the compound noun.

Examples: mother-in-law   mothers-in-law
                wineglass   wineglasses

Write the plural form of each compound noun. Use a dictionary to check the spelling.

1. **pogo stick** _____

2. **baseball** _____

3. **maitre d'hotel** _____

4. **coup d'etat** _____

5. **go-between** _____

6. **standby** _____

7. **printout** _____

8. **hanger-on** _____

Write sentences using the compound nouns *bill of sale* and *manservant* in both their singular and plural forms.

1. _____

2. _____

3. _____

4. _____

Plural Compound Nouns

Compound nouns form their plurals by adding -*s* to the most important word in the compound noun.

Examples: mother-in-law   mothers-in-law
                  wineglass   wineglasses

Write the plural form of each compound noun. Use a dictionary to check the spelling.

1. **father-in-law** _____

2. **will-o'-the-wisp** _____

3. **toothbrush** _____

4. **paintbrush** _____

5. **hand-me-down** _____

6. **good-by** _____

7. **stepmother** _____

8. **backpack** _____

Write sentences using the compound nouns *mother-in-law* and *hand-me-down* in both their singular and plural forms.

1. _____

2. _____

3. _____

4. _____

Plural Compound Nouns

Compound nouns form their plurals by adding *-s* to the most important word in the compound noun.

Examples: mother-in-law   mothers-in-law
                 wineglass   wineglasses

Write the plural form of each compound noun. Use a dictionary to check the spelling.

1. **passerby** _____

2. **time-out** _____

3. **toothbrush** _____

4. **foothold** _____

5. **talisman** _____

6. **get-together** _____

7. **two-by-four** _____

8. **handcuff** _____

Write sentences using the compound nouns *passerby* and *toothbrush* in both their singular and plural forms.

1. _____

2. _____

3. _____

4. _____

Plural Foreign Nouns

Some nouns of foreign origin that are commonly used in English retain the plural form of the language from which they came. Some use the typical English plurals *-s* and *-es*. Others have English and foreign forms.

Examples: <u>Singular</u>   <u>English</u>   <u>Foreign</u>
            vertebra   vertebras   vertebrae
            alumnus   alumni

Use a dictionary to determine the plural (or plurals) of each of the following nouns of foreign origin.

<u>Singular</u>	<u>English Plural</u>	<u>Foreign Plural</u>
1. **stimulus**	_____	_____
2. **synthesis**	_____	_____
3. **synopsis**	_____	_____
4. **emphasis**	_____	_____
5. **diagnosis**	_____	_____
6. **radius**	_____	_____
7. **datum**	_____	_____
8. **crisis**	_____	_____
9. **syllabus**	_____	_____
10. **genus**	_____	_____
11. **agendum**	_____	_____
12. **parenthesis**	_____	_____

Plural Foreign Nouns

Some nouns of foreign origin that are commonly used in English retain the plural form of the language from which they came. Some use the typical English plurals -*s* and -*es*. Others have English and foreign forms.

Examples:

Singular	English	Foreign
datum		data
tableau	tableaus	tableaux

Use a dictionary to determine the plural (or plurals) of each of the following nouns of foreign origin.

Singular	English Plural	Foreign Plural
1. matrix	_____	_____
2. paparazzo	_____	_____
3. plateau	_____	_____
4. cranium	_____	_____
5. momentum	_____	_____
6. nucleus	_____	_____
7. prospectus	_____	_____
8. antenna	_____	_____
9. formula	_____	_____
10. basis	_____	_____
11. curriculum	_____	_____
12. axis	_____	_____

Possessive Nouns

To make a singular noun **possessive**, add -*s*. If the noun ends in -*s* and is plural in meaning, add only an apostrophe. If the noun is singular in meaning, but ends in -*s*, add -'*s*.

Examples: Noun not ending in -*s*   the boy   the boy's basketball
Noun ending in -*s*   the boss   the boss's temper
Plural noun   the bosses   the bosses' meeting
Irregular Plurals   children   children's toys

An exception is made in the case of words in which an extra *s* would make pronunciation difficult such as "for goodness' sake." In that case, add only an apostrophe.

The singular form of each noun below is given. Write the other forms requested.

singular	singular possessive	plural	plural possessive
1. book	*book's*	*books*	*books'*
2. hem			
3. exercise			
4. company			
5. piano			
6. movie			
7. waitress			
8. lady			
9. dormouse			
10. life			

8

Possessive Nouns

To make a singular noun **possessive**, add -s. If the noun ends in -s and is plural in meaning, add only an apostrophe. If the noun is singular in meaning, but ends in -s, add -'s.

Examples:
Noun not ending in -s	the boy	the boy's basketball
Noun ending in -s	the boss	the boss's temper
Plural noun	the bosses	the bosses' meeting
Irregular Plurals	children	children's toys

An exception is made in the case of words in which an extra s would make pronunciation difficult such as "for goodness' sake." In that case, add only an apostrophe.

The singular form of each noun below is given. Write the other forms requested.

singular	singular possessive	plural	plural possessive
1. book	_____	_____	_____
2 costume	_____	_____	_____
3. church	_____	_____	_____
4. cloak	_____	_____	_____
5. test	_____	_____	_____
6. hurricane	_____	_____	_____
7. briefcase	_____	_____	_____
8. goose	_____	_____	_____
9. cliff	_____	_____	_____
10. fedora	_____	_____	_____

Name _____   **Pronouns**

Types of Pronouns

Pronouns take the place of nouns. There are several kinds.
1. **Personal pronouns** include forms of 1st, 2nd, and 3rd person: *I, mine, me, we, ours, us, you, yours, he, she, it, his, hers, its, him, her, they, theirs, and them.*
2. **Indefinite pronouns** refer to persons or things generally: *anybody, few, most, neither, no one, nothing, several, etc.*
3. **Demonstrative pronouns** refer to persons or things specifically: *this, that, these, and those.*
4. **Relative pronouns** connect a dependent clause to the main clause and function as the subject or object of the dependent clause: *who, which, that, whose, whom.* The ending *-ever* can be added to each form.
5. **Reflexive pronouns** are formed by adding *-self* or *-selves* to the personal pronouns (except for *himself, ourself, theirself,* and *theirselves.*) Pronouns are reflexive when the same person or thing is both the subject and object. (Intensive pronouns use the same forms, but simply emphasize a noun or pronoun without adding new meaning.)
6. **Reciprocal pronouns** express shared feelings or actions: *each other, one another.*

Read each sentence and identify the underlined word as: personal (P), indefinite (I), demonstrative (D), relative (REL), reflexive (REF), or reciprocal (REC).

_____ 1. <u>They</u> enjoyed the movie very much.

_____ 2. What did <u>she</u> say?

_____ 3. Rachel thought the purse was <u>mine</u>.

_____ 4. <u>This</u> is a group of volunteers who are indispensable.

_____ 5. Maria saw <u>herself</u> on the evening news.

_____ 6. The brothers helped <u>each other</u>.

_____ 7. Has <u>anyone</u> offered to help?

_____ 8. Joy knows <u>everyone</u> at school.

_____ 9. Who will go with <u>me</u> tonight?

Changing Nouns to Pronouns

In each sentence choose a pronoun to take the place of the underlined words and write it on the line. Choose from the following types of pronouns:
personal (PER), possessive (POS), demonstrative (DEM), indefinite (IND), and reflexive (REF).

_____ 1. Ms. Rausch asked what scene had a need for <u>the rifles</u>.
                                                                                                  (DEM)

_____ 2. <u>The entrance of the soldiers in Act I</u> was very effective.
                          (PER)

_____ 3. The soldiers were pleased with <u>their performance</u>.
                                                                 (REF)

_____ 4. Then <u>Carmen</u> made her appearance.
                          (PER)

_____ 5. The stage director kept running through <u>Act I</u> over and over.
                                                                   (PER)

_____ 6. The singers muttered objections to <u>the repeated run throughs</u>.
                                                                            (DEM)

_____ 7. The urchins were not comfortable with their music yet, but the school girls in Act IV were comfortable with <u>the part</u>.
                                                                                            (POS)

_____ 8. <u>The members of the chorus</u> sounded terrific.
                        (IND)

_____ 9. An entrance down the stairs was made by <u>the cigarette girls</u>.
                                                                              (PER)

_____ 10. <u>The choral and stage directors</u> were working twelve hour days.
                        (PER)

_____ 11. The principals were pleased with <u>their performance</u>.
                                                              (REF)

_____ 12. The audience gave <u>the performers</u> a standing ovation.
                                                       (PER)

Name _____

Auxiliary Verbs

Auxiliary verbs, also called helping verbs, always accompany a main verb. An auxiliary verb helps the main verb to express tense, voice, or mood, but usually has little meaning of its own. Some examples include *be, do, have, can, might, would, may, will,* and *must.* If an auxiliary verb is used alone, it is not an auxiliary verb in that sentence. A combination of two or more verbs is called a verb phrase. Verb phrases contain at least one auxiliary verb. Adverbs may appear in the middle of a verb phrase, but are not part of it.

Examples:　　We <u>are waiting</u> in a long line.
　　　　　　　I <u>did go</u> with him.
　　　　　　　I <u>would have gone</u>.
　　　　　　　I <u>have been walking</u>.
　　　　　　　I <u>could</u> hardly <u>wait</u>.

Underline the main verb once.　Underline the auxiliary verb(s) twice.

1. **Elmer has rarely exhibited a bad temper.**

2. **The county will try the case next month.**

3. **The man had received no driver's license.**

4. **I could not complete the task in that length of time.**

5. **Those girls are known as the Baxter twins.**

6. **The cat was playing with the drapery cord.**

7. **The popularity of that product has risen for months.**

8. **The Empire State Building was used as a set in many famous movies.**

9. **The Twin Towers is now dominating the New York skyline.**

10. **We will begin the long drive early in the morning.**

11. **I have been jogging with Alex for two years.**

12. **Do you know the coach?**

Name _____   **Verbs**

Linking Verbs

Linking verbs describe conditions instead of actions. They are followed by words that rename or describe the subject. Forms of the verb *to be* are most commonly used as linking verbs. Some other verbs used as linking verbs are *appear, become, feel, grow, look, prove, remain, seem,* and *turn.* These verbs do not function as linking verbs if they do not describe conditions that are followed by a word that renames or describes the subject.

Examples: Carla <u>is</u> my only sister. (linking)
Carla's friend <u>is</u> running for governor. (auxiliary)
Bob <u>grew</u> sleepy during the long lecture. (linking)
Roger <u>grew</u> beautiful roses in his garden. (action)

Read each sentence. If the verb is linking, write L in the blank. If the verb is not linking, write NL.

_____ 1. The roar of the sea <u>was</u> imposing.

_____ 2. The roar of the sea <u>was</u> <u>heard</u> far away.

_____ 3. Mandy <u>looks</u> pretty in pink.

_____ 4. Mandy <u>looked</u> behind the sofa for the remote.

_____ 5. Valerie <u>appeared</u> on a local television show last night.

_____ 6. Valerie <u>appeared</u> anxious about her exam.

_____ 7. Jennifer <u>felt</u> uncomfortable with the new crowd.

_____ 8. Jennifer <u>felt</u> the child's feverish forehead.

_____ 9. The wasp nest <u>is</u> near the door.

_____10. The wasp nest <u>is</u> a scary sight to the child.

_____11. Evacuation plans <u>were</u> <u>devised</u> in advance of the hurricane.

_____12. The evacuation plans <u>were</u> unclear.

Irregular Verbs

The principle parts of a verb are the three forms upon which all tenses are based.

<u>Present</u>	<u>Past</u>	<u>Past Participle</u> (auxiliary verb needed)
love	loved	loved

Many frequently used verbs have principle parts that are irregularly formed.

<u>Present</u>	<u>Past</u>	<u>Past Participle</u> (auxiliary verb needed)
drive	drove	driven

Look at the present form of the verb given. Fill in the other two forms. Use a dictionary to check your work.

<u>Present</u>	**<u>Past</u>**	**<u>Past Participle</u>**
1. lay	_____	_____
2. speak	_____	_____
3. forsake	_____	_____
4. lie	_____	_____
5. begin	_____	_____
6. rise	_____	_____
7. swear	_____	_____
8. fly	_____	_____
9. slay	_____	_____
10. grind	_____	_____
11. shake	_____	_____
12. string	_____	_____

Irregular Verbs

The principle parts of a verb include present (infinitive), past and past participle. Regular verbs form the past tense by adding -*ed,* and the past participle form by adding -*ed* plus at least one auxiliary verb. **Irregular verbs** form the past and past participle in ways other than -*ed*, although the past participle must still be used with one or more auxiliary verbs.

Example: <u>Infinitive</u>   <u>Past</u>   <u>Past Participle</u>
                to drive   drove   driven

Write the irregular verb form that is requested in each of the following sentences. P indicates that past is requested, and PP indicates that the past participle is requested.

1. draw (PP)—Elizabeth had _____ a geometric design on her notebook.

2. forgive (P)—Jo _____ Amy for burning her manuscript.

3. do (PP)—Russell had _____ his homework before he went to the movie.

4. write (P)—William Golding _____ *Lord of the Flies.*

5. tear (PP)—The toddler has _____ her favorite book.

6. wind (P)—The path _____ around the lake.

7. swear (P)—The witness _____ that he would tell the truth.

8. set (PP)—I had _____ the clock properly, but the electricity went out.

9. ring (PP)—The bell had _____ before Stacey got off the bus.

10. ride (P)—Lauren _____ the gentle mare on the beach.

Simple Verb Tense

The **tense** of the verb shows the time of an action. The simple **present tense** shows that an action takes place now at the same time that it is being described. It is also used to describe habitual action, to tell general truths, or to write about books, movies, and other narratives. It can also be used to indicate a time in the future. The **past tense** shows that an action took place at some previous time. The **future tense** shows the action will take place at some time to come.

Examples: The child <u>fills</u> her dog's bowl daily with fresh water. (present)
                   The people <u>elect</u> their government in a democratic society. (present)
                   I <u>leave</u> for Costa Rica tomorrow. (present)
                   He <u>filled</u> the glasses and everyone toasted. (past)
                   Jenny <u>will fill</u> the garden with bright flowers. (future)

Underline the complete verb. Determine the tense (present, past, or future) and write it on the line provided.

_____ 1. The family frequents the beach all summer.

_____ 2. I see a wide variety of flora and fauna at the wildlife preserve.

_____ 3. In the musical *The Secret Garden*, Mary Lennox sings with Archibald Dickon and the ghost of Lilly.

_____ 4. The city finally started a recycling program.

_____ 5. These opera glasses will really help you see the performance.

_____ 6. Drew misplaced the portable phone again.

_____ 7. We danced until the clock struck midnight.

_____ 8. The dog will not bite someone as nice as you.

_____ 9. The network will broadcast the game live on Saturday night.

_____ 10. The washing machine repairman is finally here.

Present Perfect Tense

The **present perfect tense** shows that an action began in the past and extends to the present or is completed in the present.

Examples: I <u>am filling</u> all the glasses. (simple present)
I <u>have filled</u> all the water glasses. (present perfect)

Jane runs three miles every day. (simple present)
Jane has run three miles every day for two weeks. (present perfect)

Read each sentence and determine its tense. Write SP in the blank for simple present or PP for present perfect.

_____ 1. **Harry washes the car on Thursdays.**

_____ 2. **Maude has seen that movie many times.**

_____ 3. **I go to the dentist twice a year.**

_____ 4. **I have been going to the dentist twice a year for quite some time now.**

_____ 5. **Jane has written an article for the school newspaper.**

_____ 6. **I have known her since she was a child.**

_____ 7. **We have three kittens.**

_____ 8. **I have had two colds this year so far.**

_____ 9. **He has taken the last bite.**

_____10. **Today is my birthday.**

_____11. **The cat is in the tree.**

_____12. **She has studied for the test all weekend.**

Past Perfect Tense

The **past perfect tense** shows that an action was completed before another action in the past or completed before a definite time in the past. It is formed by using *had* and the past participle form of the verb.

Example: I <u>had run</u> five miles a day before the jogging accident.

Read each sentence. Underline the complete verb. If the tense of the verb is past perfect, write PP in the blank.

_____ 1. Jeanette has frequented the mall since she was thirteen.

_____ 2. Jeanette frequented the mall after school.

_____ 3. Jeanette had frequented the mall until her mother took her credit cards.

_____ 4. The old woman walked with difficulty.

_____ 5. The old woman had walked with difficulty for years.

_____ 6. The train ran late.

_____ 7. The train had run late on that fateful night.

_____ 8. That train has run late often.

_____ 9. The graffiti had been unsightly on the subway walls until the walls were freshly painted.

_____10. The graffiti has covered the subway walls of Paris for years.

Rewrite the following sentences in the past perfect tense.

1. I have known the waiter at Brennan's for years.

   _____

2. Ralph attended Clearwater High School.

   _____

Future Perfect Tense

The **future perfect tense** shows that an action will be completed in the future before another action in the future or before a given time in the future. The future perfect combines the auxiliary verbs *will* and *have* with the past participle of the main verb.

Example: The jury will convict the defendant. (simple future)
                         They <u>will have convicted</u> the defendant by now. (future perfect)

Put a check in the blank before each sentence that is in the future perfect tense.

_____ 1. **By next year Roger and Patricia will have built their own log cabin.**

_____ 2. **They will continue to try to stop you from making mistakes.**

_____ 3. **In a few years the Octogenarian Club will have been decimated.**

_____ 4. **Roger and Patricia will build a log cabin as a summer home.**

_____ 5. **The squirrels will collect a supply of nuts throughout the orchard.**

_____ 6. **Andrew will have returned home by 11 o'clock.**

Write each of the following sentences in the future perfect tense. Be sure to connect each to another event in the future or a specified time.

1. **The baby will eat solid food.**

   _____

   _____

2. **The group of girls will walk to the mall.**

   _____

   _____

Progressive Form

All verb tenses have a progressive form. The **progressive form** combines an auxiliary verb with the present participle form of the verb which ends in -*ing*. This form emphasizes continuing action or action in progress.

Examples: I <u>am running</u> more often now. (present progressive)
He <u>was running</u> when he saw Alice. (past progressive)
I <u>will be running</u> every Tuesday. (future progressive)
I <u>have been running</u> all summer. (present perfect progressive)
He <u>had been running</u> for years until his injury. (past perfect progressive)
She <u>will have been taking</u> ballet lessons for 10 years before becoming a teaching assistant. (future perfect progressive)

Identify each of the following sentences by the letter of the correct progressive form. If the form is not progressive, write NP.

A) present progressive   D) present perfect progressive
B) past progressive   E) past perfect progressive
C) future progressive   F) future perfect progressive

_____ 1. Janet <u>was looking</u> in the phone directory for an auto repair shop.

_____ 2. The librarian <u>will be waiting</u> for you to finish the make-up exam.

_____ 3. I <u>am taking</u> advanced English this year.

_____ 4. Greg <u>had been looking</u> forward to the prom, until his date got the flu.

_____ 5. The manager <u>has been working</u> with the employees to boost sales.

_____ 6. By June, Elaine <u>will have been volunteering</u> at the hospital for fifteen years.

_____ 7. Babies <u>were crawling</u> all over the room at the day care center.

_____ 8. I <u>am going</u> to your house today.

_____ 9. Meghan <u>has found</u> the right canopy for her bed.

_____ 10. The child <u>has been refusing</u> to eat green peas for years.

Verb Tense Review

Read the sentences and underline the complete verb for each. Select the letter of the correct verb tense and write it on the line before each sentence.

A. Simple Present   G. Present Progressive
B. Simple Past   H. Past Progressive
C. Simple Future   I. Future Progressive
D. Present Perfect   J. Present Perfect Progressive
E. Past Perfect   K. Past Perfect Progressive
F. Future Perfect   L. Future Perfect Progressive

_____ 1. She was watering the garden too much.

_____ 2. Nick will have been teaching for fifteen years by the time he retires..

_____ 3. The leading lady had not missed one rehearsal since January.

_____ 4. I will have graduated by the year 2025.

_____ 5. Jody is dragging his dog away from the cat.

_____ 6. Students will be using calculators for complex math problems.

_____ 7. I have been doing my best with this project.

_____ 8. I will think about that comment.

_____ 9. Give me a break.

_____ 10. We had been playing soccer when she fell and broke her leg.

_____ 11. The weather has been a factor in our plans.

_____ 12. Had you studied hard for that test?

_____ 13. The students were studying for the test during lunch.

_____ 14. Jack located the most foreign phrases for the assignment.

Verb Tense Review

Rewrite the following sentences in the tense requested.

1. **Rafael will be arriving by plane at 6 o'clock.**
   (change to present progressive)

   _____

2. **Mark had avoided his friend all afternoon.**
   (change to present progressive)

   _____

3. **Manuel tended the garden with loving care.**
   (change to simple future)

   _____

4. **Adam was snoring loudly on the couch all afternoon.**
   (change to present perfect)

   _____

5. **Margot and Jack will have been dating for two years on Valentine's Day.**
   (change to past perfect progressive)

   _____

6. **The thief has been caught with the cookie in her hand.**
   (change to simple past)

   _____

7. **I will be happy to go with you.**
   (change to simple present)

   _____

Verb Tense Review

Write a sentence with the verb given in the tense indicated.

1. (to run—past perfect) _____

_____

2. (to see—simple present) _____

_____

3. (to go—future progressive) _____

_____

4. (to drive—past progressive) _____

_____

5. (to help—simple past) _____

_____

6. (to smile—future perfect) _____

_____

7. (to fall—simple future) _____

_____

8. (to work—present perfect) _____

_____

9. (to swim—future progressive) _____

_____

Transitive and Intransitive Verbs

The classification of verbs is directly related to how they function with subjects and objects. **Transitive verbs** require a direct object to complete their meanings. If the question "Who?" or "What?" can be answered after an action verb, the verb is transitive. **Intransitive verbs** express an action that is complete in itself and are often followed by a prepositional phrase. Some verbs can be used as either transitive or intransitive. Linking verbs are never transitive.

Examples: The race <u>began</u>. (Intransitive)
                 Meghan <u>began</u> *The Giver* last week. (Transitive)
                 The feature <u>began</u> at 3 o'clock. (Intransitive)
                 She <u>is</u> the winner. (Intransitive)

For each sentence below, circle the transitive verbs and underline the intransitive verbs.

1. Betty ate the whole pie.

2. The teacher wanted the answer too quickly.

3. Chloe is a citizen of the United States.

4. Salvador described the diamond brooch in great detail.

5. The cat always slept under the bed.

6. The content of the editorial was unsettling.

7. The Belgian man married an Egyptian women.

8. The evidence is compelling in this case.

9. The Morrison family lives in the suburbs.

10. Allison understood the concept very well.

11. Mark ran into a problem at work today.

12. Mark ran five miles every morning.

Active and Passive Verbs

A verb is **active** when the subject is the doer of the action. A verb is **passive** when the subject is the receiver of the action.

Example: The fireman <u>rescued</u> the baby from the burning building. (active)
The baby <u>was rescued</u> from the burning building. (passive)

Identify each sentence as active (A) or passive (P). If it is active, rewrite it as passive. If it is passive, rewrite it as active.

_____ 1. The prescription was filled by the pharmacist.

_____

_____ 2. The children pitied the stray dog.

_____

_____ 3. The proceeds from the fundraiser were deposited by the treasurer.

_____

_____ 4. Cedrick left a message on my voice mail.

_____

_____ 5. The movie critic reviewed the new release.

_____

_____ 6. My brother ordered salad as an appetizer.

_____

_____ 7. The audience applauded the tenor's solo.

_____

Name _____ **Verbs**

Active and Passive Verbs

A verb is **active** when the subject is the doer of the action. A verb is **passive** when the subject is the receiver of the action.

Examples: The fireman <u>rescued</u> the baby from the burning building. (active)
                      The baby <u>was rescued</u> from the burning building. (passive)

Identify each sentence as active (A) or passive (P).

_____ 1. Perry believed the tall tale.

_____ 2. The small craft sank in the storm.

_____ 3. Clothilde waited for the signal.

_____ 4. The banana split was devoured by the young child.

_____ 5. The short story was written by an eighth grader.

_____ 6. The wind damaged the roof of the garage.

_____ 7. The honest person returned my wallet.

_____ 8. My wallet was returned by the honest person.

_____ 9. The son was running the business now.

_____ 10. The business was run by the youngest son.

_____ 11. The rumor was denied by her classmates.

_____ 12. Her classmates denied the rumor.

_____ 13. The purse was found in the cloakroom.

_____ 14. The janitor found the missing purse.

_____ 15. The Red Cross aided the flood victims.

Descriptive, Limiting, and Pronominal Adjectives

An **adjective** modifies a noun (or pronoun). There are several kinds. **Descriptive adjectives** describe or characterize a noun by making the meaning more precise. There are also two kinds of limiting **adjectives** called definite and indefinite articles. The indefinite article *the* specifies a particular noun. The indefinite articles *a* and *an* generalize the noun. Adjectives derived from pronoun forms are called **pronominal adjectives**.

Examples: shabby couch (descriptive)   the truth (limiting)
Catholic priest (descriptive)   a sign (limiting)
this time (pronominal)   an apple (limiting)
which direction (pronominal)   some days (pronominal)
its cover (pronominal)

Underline each adjective and classify it as D for descriptive, L for limiting, or P for pronominal. The first one has been done for you.

1. The __African__ safari took us through __a__ __magnificent__ __wildlife__ preserve.

2. Amy wore a white blouse with a straight skirt and wide belt.

3. Whose picture is in the newspaper?

4. The choice of colors was a big mistake.

5. Every girl in the room was over thirteen.

6. The May flood will not soon be forgotten by New Orleans residents.

7. Some people had eighteen inches of water in their houses.

8. I can't decide which luscious dessert to choose.

9. The flamenco dancer was appearing nightly in Granada.

10. I can't decide which computer to choose for home use.

11. Her father muttered about the outrageous prices of school textbooks.

12. The cab which we liked best was driven by an older man.

Predicate Adjectives

Adjectives that describe the subject, but follow the linking verb are called **predicate adjectives**.

Example: The designer purse is <u>expensive</u>. (predicate adjective)

Designer and *expensive* both describe the purse. Notice that *designer* is a descriptive adjective because it precedes the noun it describes, and *expensive* is a predicate adjective because it comes after the subject and follows a linking verb.

Read each sentence. Underline each descriptive adjective and circle each predicate adjective.

1. Her cherished scrapbook was filled with special mementos.

2. Malcolm's actions were inexcusable.

3. The weary soldier looked excited at the thought of rest.

4. The chocolate cake was scrumptious.

5. Sharon bought her school supplies at the last minute.

6. The classroom dictionary was worn.

7. The rambunctious cat tangled the curtain cords.

8. The wildlife calendar was stunning.

9. Jack is a successful architect.

10. The crystal vase shattered on the marble floor.

11. The teacher became annoyed with the noise level.

12. The kindergartner looked angelic, but was not.

Pronominal Adjectives

Pronominal adjectives are pronouns that are used as adjectives. Demonstrative forms (*this, that, these,* and *those*) refer to objects that have already been mentioned or can be pointed out. Interrogative forms such as *what, which,* and *whose* modify a noun in the context of a question. Relative forms such as *whose* or *which* introduce a subordinate clause and modify a noun in the clause. Indefinite forms such as *any, some, every, each, other, neither,* and *both* modify a noun in a nonspecific way. Possessive forms such as *my, your, his, her, their,* and *its* show possession of the noun that follows.

Examples: <u>This</u> booksack is worn. (demonstrative)
      <u>What</u> time did you arrive? (interrogative)
      Choose <u>which</u> color you like. (relative)
      <u>Each</u> selection looked intriguing. (indefinite)
      He felt the sting of <u>her</u> words. (possessive)

Look at the italicized pronominal adjective in each sentence and classify it as demonstrative (D), interrogative (INT), relative (REL), indefinite (IND), or possessive (PO).

_____ 1. *Your* hair needs brushing.

_____ 2. *Which* brother is the handsome one?

_____ 3. *Whose* book is on the table?

_____ 4. Do you have *any* fax paper?

_____ 5. *Their* noses were really sunburned.

_____ 6. *These* Belgian chocolates are delectable.

_____ 7. *Whose* picture is in your locker?

_____ 8. Valerie didn't know *which* invitation arrived first.

_____ 9. *Neither* day is good for me.

_____10. I couldn't find *those* scissors in my sewing box.

Comparison Adjectives

The three degrees of comparison of adjectives are **positive**, **comparative**, and **superlative**. The comparative degree shows the relationship between two persons, objects, or ideas. The superlative degree shows the relationship among three or more. The change is commonly indicated by the endings -er and -est in one syllable adjectives. *More* and *most* or *less* and *least* are used to form comparatives and superlatives when adjectives contain more than two syllables. Some adjectives that contain two syllables can form comparisons either way, but some can only use *more* and *most* or *less* and *least*.

Examples:

Positive	Comparative	Superlative
small	smaller	smallest
narrow	narrower	narrowest
handsome	more handsome	most handsome

Fill in the blank with the correct comparative form of the adjective.

1. (high) One of the towers was _____ than the other.

2. (practical) His suggestion was the _____ of all the solutions.

3. (wise) The adage was _____ than his friends' advice.

4. (rapid) The noon train was _____ than any of the others.

5. (thick) Melba chose the _____ novel of the two.

6. (cheap) This model of the appliance is the _____.

7. (handsome) Harold is _____ than his brother.

8. (adventurous) Mark is _____ than his brother Mike.

9. (distinct) The print on this copy is the _____ of any of them.

10. (modest) This bathing suit is _____ than that one.

Irregular Comparisons

Some adjectives are not logically capable of comparison in formal speech and writing because their meaning is **absolute** (e.g., fatal, complete, etc.), although some of these can be modified by adverbs such as *more, less, nearly,* or *virtually*.

Example: Jasmine's design was even <u>more</u> unique.

Look at each adjective. If it can be generally compared by degree, write C. If it is usually an absolute, write A.

_____ 1. empty	_____ 9. exotic	_____ 17. infinite
_____ 2. kind	_____ 10. perfect	_____ 18. pious
_____ 3. final	_____ 11. sturdy	_____ 19. weird
_____ 4. remote	_____ 12. promising	_____ 20. fine
_____ 5. serene	_____ 13. round	_____ 21. skillful
_____ 6. complete	_____ 14. universal	_____ 22. efficient
_____ 7. lovely	_____ 15. correct	_____ 23. wrong
_____ 8. evil	_____ 16. eternal	_____ 24. single

Choose 5 absolutes and write a sentence with each one.

1. _____

2. _____

3. _____

4. _____

5. _____

Adjective Review

In each sentence, look at the underlined adjective. Write what type of adjective it is in the blank. Use the following abbreviations:

(D) demonstrative　　**(I) interrogative**　　**(R) relative**
(IND) indefinite　　　**(P) possessive**　　　**(DES) descriptive**

_____ 1. <u>This</u> book is so interesting.

_____ 2. <u>That</u> is the girl who won the math contest.

_____ 3. I don't know <u>which</u> pencil to use.

_____ 4. I saw a really <u>scary</u> movie late last night.

_____ 5. <u>My</u> big sister helps me with my homework.

_____ 6. <u>Whose</u> sweater is this?

_____ 7. Is <u>this</u> play going to last much longer?

_____ 8. He has a <u>big</u> head.

_____ 9. <u>Each</u> person should bring his own lunch.

_____ 10. I love this little <u>white</u> kitten.

_____ 11. I want <u>this</u> bike for my birthday.

_____ 12. <u>Your</u> hair is a mess.

_____ 13. <u>Their</u> way is the wrong way.

_____ 14. <u>Neither</u> one is what I really want.

_____ 15. <u>Which</u> night is good for you?

Adverbs

An **adverb** is a word used to modify a verb, adjective, or another adverb. Some adverbs are formed from adjectives and simply add -*ly,* but many do not. Adverbs answer a variety of questions about the word they modify including *How*, *How often*, *To what degree*, *When*, and *Where*. An adverb can be a single word, a phrase, or a clause.

Examples: The volunteers worked <u>selflessly</u>. (how)
                          I return to my hometown <u>occasionally</u>. (how often)
                          She seemed <u>very</u> knowledgeable. (to what degree)
                          You can go <u>tomorrow</u>. (when)
                          He travels <u>everywhere</u>. (where)

A simple adverb is underlined in each sentence. Circle the word it modifies. Identify the word it modifies as a verb (V), adjective (ADJ), or another adverb (ADV).

_____ 1. Playing the guitar was <u>much</u> too difficult for the five year old.

_____ 2. That scheming opportunist was <u>once</u> my friend.

_____ 3. Please give a <u>very</u> generous donation to the fundraiser for Children's Hospital.

_____ 4. A unicycle has <u>only</u> one wheel.

_____ 5. The students from Washington Junior High visit the library <u>regularly</u>.

_____ 6. I saw him <u>once</u>, and it was unforgettable.

_____ 7. Vinnie <u>always</u> jogs in Central Park on the weekend.

_____ 8. The national debt is becoming <u>increasingly</u> important to the electorate.

_____ 9. The hot dogs burned <u>quickly</u> on the barbecue pit.

_____ 10. The snow goose flew <u>east</u>.

Intensifiers

Adverbs usually modify the verb by telling *where, when, how, to what degree,* and *under what conditions.* Adjectives modify or describe nouns and pronouns. Adverbs that modify other adverbs or adjectives are called **intensifiers**.

Examples: Matt fell <u>very</u> awkwardly to the ground.
                       She is a <u>really</u> pretty girl.

Underline the intensifier. If it modifies an adverb, write ADV in the blank. If it modifies an adjective, write ADJ.

_____ 1. Scarlet O'Hara's waist was exceptionally small.

_____ 2. The phone rang most frequently between five and six.

_____ 3. The message sounded extremely urgent.

_____ 4. Curry is a spice quite commonly found in Indian food.

_____ 5. The very tired runner collapsed.

_____ 6. Virginia had a really suspicious look on her face.

_____ 7. His mood changed too quickly.

_____ 8. The winner acted rather conceited.

_____ 9. The storyteller always told completely unbelievable tales.

_____10. The speech was exceedingly tedious.

_____11. The beach was extraordinarily hot.

_____12. I can come almost any time.

_____13. She is somewhat smarter in trigonometry than Ralph.

_____14. The situation grew increasingly desperate.

_____15. Jeff complained about the absolutely awful movie.

Name _____   **Prepositions**

Identifying Prepositions

Prepositions connect nouns and pronouns to other words in a sentence and show their relationship. Prepositions never stand alone. They introduce a prepositional phrase that contains a noun or pronoun and its modifiers.

Examples: spoon *under* the kitchen table
                         morning *before* the wedding
                         bird *in* the sycamore tree

Fill in the blank with a preposition. Underline the phrase it introduces.

1. The memorable part was sung _____ the amazing tenor.

2. The inconspicuous woman _____ the blue dress
    shoplifted an expensive watch.

3. Baton Rouge Is the capital _____ Louisiana.

4. The coffee _____ Brazil was the most aromatic.

5. The rest _____ the ice cream mysteriously disappeared.

6. The book was _____ the War of the Roses.

7. The shutters rattled loudly _____ the storm.

8. The whole class is going _____ the teacher.

9. The news spread _____ the countryside.

10. No one knew what was _____ those mountains.

11. The remote was firmly lodged _____ the cushions.

12. I wondered what was happening _____ the huddle.

13. The unearthly noise _____ the house unnerved everyone.

14. The telephone message _____ Kevin's delayed arrival
     was not delivered.

Prepositional Phrases as Adjectives and Adverbs

A **prepositional phrase** functions like an adjective when it describes a noun in a sentence. A prepositional phrase functions like an adverb when it modifies a verb in a sentence.

Examples: The police hurried _to_ the scene. (prepositional phrase as adverb)
                   The girl _in_ pink is my older sister. (prepositional phrase as adjective)

Underline the prepositional phrase in each sentence. Fill in the blank with adjective (ADJ) or adverb (ADV) as appropriate.

_____ 1. A caterpillar crawled up the stalk.

_____ 2. The train to Nuremberg was late.

_____ 3. The room to the left is the guest bedroom.

_____ 4. Andre fell in the mud puddle.

_____ 5. The mail should arrive at two o'clock.

_____ 6. The key is in my purse.

_____ 7. He ate a piece of my cookie.

_____ 8. Fabienne hid behind the palm tree.

_____ 9. Who is the woman with the red hair?

_____10. The flowers on the back porch need watering.

_____11. My sister works in the Central Business District.

_____12. It will undoubtedly rain before morning.

_____13. I bought a car with a sun roof.

_____14. The ferry to Giglio sails hourly.

_____15. This pottery is from the Yucatan Peninsula.

Prepositions

Changing Prepositional Phrases

Underline the prepositional phrase in each sentence. Rewrite the sentence changing the prepositional phrase to a possessive noun.

Example: The cost *of* the ticket seemed excessive.
                 The ticket's cost seemed excessive.

1. The reunion of the sisters was a tearjerker.

   _____

2. The ending of the novel was a big disappointment.

   _____

3. The intentions of Carmen are very clear.

   _____

4. The weight of her suitcase was incredible.

   _____

5. The recipe of Josephine makes the absolute best oyster dressing.

   _____

6. Mr. Travis lived the life of a hermit.

   _____

7. The performance of the diva was a big disappointment.

   _____

8. The actions of Stephanie were heartless.

   _____

9. The portrait of Tim was an oil painting.

   _____

10. The pet of the teacher could not win a popularity contest.

   _____

Prepositional Phrases

Change the following phrases consisting of a noun and its modifiers to a prepositional phrase describing the noun.

Example: a jungle animal
             an animal *of* the jungle

1. **the Swahili language** _____

2. **the cheerleading squad** _____

3. **the precipice's edge** _____

4. **the flawed account** _____

5. **the unexpected discovery** _____

6. **the garden path** _____

7. **the painful look** _____

8. **the freckled nose** _____

9. **the mournful sound** _____

10. **the isolated retreat** _____

11. **the wrought iron chairs** _____

12. **the Chilean flag** _____

13. **the red-haired woman** _____

14. **the intensely hot summer** _____

15. **the renowned playwright** _____

Coordinating Conjunctions

Conjunctions join words or groups of words. One kind of conjunction is a coordinating conjunction. **Coordinating conjunctions** connect single words, phrases, and clauses that are of the same importance or rank. The most common coordinating conjunctions are *and, but, or, nor, yet, for,* and *so. Nor* is only used in negative sentences.

Examples:
The children feasted on cookies <u>and</u> milk. (joins words)
The kids asked me to come <u>and</u> join them. (joins phrases)
I can go, <u>but</u> you can't. (joins clauses or simple sentences)
Roses need drainage, <u>or</u> their leaves turn yellow. (joins clauses)
I never eat fast food <u>nor</u> candy. (joins words)

Read each sentence. Supply an appropriate coordinating conjunction. Write on the line if it is joining words (W), phrases (P), or clauses (C).

_____ 1. There are two trails in the rain forest, _____ hikers can choose a short or long walk.

_____ 2. I intellectually agree _____ emotionally disagree with your decision.

_____ 3. The child never sees movies rated PG-13 _____ R.

_____ 4. The work was hard _____ satisfying.

_____ 5. The lights were dimmed _____ the play began.

_____ 6. I must buy this painting, _____ it will look terrific in my living room.

_____ 7. Will you attend the party given by Melba _____ Mable?

_____ 8. Did you finish your homework _____ did you fall asleep?

_____ 9. The child can ride the bike _____ not climb the tree.

_____10. Sloths _____ iguanas abound in Costa Rica.

Correlative Conjunctions

Conjunctions join words or groups of words. **Correlative conjunctions** are paired connective words that link single words, phrases (combinations of words that go together within sentences), and clauses (word combinations containing subjects and predicates). The correlative conjunctions are:

both .... and	neither ... nor	whether .... or
either .... or	not only ... but (also)	

Example: She has met <u>neither</u> Polly <u>nor</u> Renee. (joins words)
She can prepare <u>either</u> an outline <u>or</u> an overview. (joins phrases)
I don't know <u>whether</u> Peter will go <u>or</u> Jack will. (joins clauses)

Read each sentence and write the appropriate correlative conjunctions in the blanks provided. Write W in the blank if the correlative conjunctions join words, P for phrases, or C for clauses.

_____ 1. He _____ documents everything, _____ keeps copies.

_____ 2. He eats _____ fish _____ chicken.

_____ 3. A healthy lifestyle includes _____ a good diet _____ a regular exercise routine.

_____ 4. _____ fat _____ sugar should appear so regularly in your lunch box.

_____ 5. _____ the fierce wind _____ the relentless rain damaged his property.

_____ 6. _____ October _____ March is the best time to visit Europe.

_____ 7. _____ the regional tourist office _____ the tour operator had the information we requested.

_____ 8. _____ get off the phone now, _____ you will not use it the rest of the week.

Subordinating Conjunctions

Conjunctions join words, phrases, or clauses. **Subordinating conjunctions** join subordinate (dependent) clauses to main (independent clauses). Subordinate clauses contain a subject and predicate, but do not stand alone as a complete thought. Main clauses can stand alone. Subordinating conjunctions clarify meaning about time, possibility, comparison, location, and cause and effect. Common subordinating conjunctions include: *after, as, before, once, till, until, when, whenever, while, as if, as though, if, unless, whether, although, than, though, how, where, wherever, because, since, whereas,* and *why*.

Examples: <u>When</u> you get here, we will begin immediately. (time)
            <u>If</u> you do not call him by tonight, you will miss your chance. (possibility)
            <u>Although</u> they look similar, ravens and crows are different. (comparison)
            I will follow you <u>wherever</u> you go. (location)
            <u>Because</u> rain was threatening, we postponed the barbecue. (cause/effect)

Read the two simple sentences. Make them into one sentence by adding a subordinating conjunction to the sentence.

Example: He saw her. He fell in love.
                  When he saw her, he fell in love.

1. **I whistle. I work.**

   _____

2. **No records were kept. No evidence remains.**

   _____

3. **Mary had her first swimming lesson. She became more confident.**

   _____

4. **The howler monkey was timid. He took the banana from my hand.**

   _____

5. **Elaine walks her dog. All the dogs in the neighborhood bark.**

   _____

6. **It is summer time. The grass grows faster.**

   _____

Name _____ **Conjunctions**

Subordinating Conjunctions

Read the two simple sentences. Make them into one sentence by adding a subordinating conjunction to the sentence.

Examples:
Tourists go to Costa Rica to see the Arenal Volcano. It often has small eruptions.
Tourists go to Costa Rica to see the Arenal Volcano *because* it often has small eruptions.
Rhoda was gone. Her rival took advantage of the situation.
While Rhoda was gone, her rival took advantage of the situation.

1. **Rita did not get the lead. She chose not to be in the play.**

   _____

2. **Valerie couldn't go. Jim didn't want to go.**

   _____

3. **We'll postpone our trip to Hong Kong. We will have more spending money.**

   _____

4. **Peggy was prettier. Dottie had a better personality.**

   _____

5. **The runner-up can become Miss America. The winner abdicates the throne.**

   _____

6. **Give me some of your cookies. I'll give you some of my popcorn.**

   _____

7. **Janet will talk to Jim. He must apologize.**

   _____

8. **We are going to New England. The leaves change.**

   _____

Interjections

Interjections express some emotion, but have no grammatical connection to the sentence. They can be followed by a comma or an exclamation point. Some commonly used interjections include: *Oh, Darn, Great, Aha, Wow, Ouch, Yech, Shh, Hey,* and *Whew.*

Example: Oh, so there you are!
                  Darn! I left my umbrella at home.

Add an interjection to each sentence.

1. _____! That really hurts.

2. _____, I got an A on the exam!

3. _____, I see.

4. _____, we have enough money to buy the VCR.

5. _____! I hate broccoli.

6. _____, watch where you're going!

7. _____, it's so hot.

8. _____, you look terrific in that dress!

9. _____! The teacher is coming.

10. _____, the sky is falling!

11. _____! Do you expect me to believe that?

12. _____, I get it.

13. _____, there's a steep drop here.

14. _____, I've finally finished.

15. _____! It's raining again.

Review

Identify the underlined part of speech in each sentence. These include noun (N), pronoun (PRO), verb (V), adjective (ADJ), adverb (ADV), conjunction (C), preposition (PRE), and interjection (INT).

_____ 1. *Les Miserables* was written <u>by</u> Victor Hugo.

_____ 2. Hugo was an influential writer in France in the nineteenth <u>century</u>.

_____ 3. Judith, have <u>you</u> seen *Les Miserables* on Broadway or in London?

_____ 4. Jean Valjean <u>is</u> the protagonist.

_____ 5. Do you consider Javert or Thernardier to be the <u>real</u> villain?

_____ 6. Jean Valjean went to prison for a total of nineteen years <u>because</u> he stole a loaf of bread and then tried to escape from prison.

_____ 7. Mayor Madeleine was an <u>alias</u> for Jean Valjean.

_____ 8. Javert pursued Jean Valjean <u>with</u> a vengeance.

_____ 9. Thernardier bargained <u>craftily</u> to make a dishonest profit.

_____10. Marius exhibited great <u>loyalty</u> to the revolutionaries in the novel.

_____11. Marius and Cosette fell <u>madly</u> in love.

_____12. Eponine felt <u>unrequited</u> love for Marius.

_____13. Azelma and Eponine were treated well by their mother, <u>but</u> Gavroche was not.

_____14. The bishop was the <u>most</u> influential person in Valjean's life.

_____15. Cosette spent <u>about</u> five years in a convent school in Paris.

_____16. Cosette and Valjean <u>often</u> strolled in the Luxembourg Gardens in the spring.

Sentence Patterns

Subject Verb (S-V)

Most sentences belong to one of five basic types. The simplest consists of a noun, pronoun, or noun phrase serving as the **subject, followed by a verb** (SV). Modifiers add information or interest to the sentence pattern without changing it.

Examples: Babies sleep. (S-V)
                 The tiny babies sleep blissfully in their sturdy cribs. (S-V)

Read each sentence. Write SV if the sentence fits this pattern. Underline the subject once and the verb twice. Write *no* if the sentence does not have the SV pattern.

_____ 1. The tall girl in the red dress left early.

_____ 2. We took the latest flight to Pensacola on Friday afternoon.

_____ 3. The dictionary sat on the desk.

_____ 4. The band played in the afternoon.

_____ 5. The plane landed.

_____ 6. Show me.

_____ 7. The approaching train blew its whistle.

_____ 8. The naughty pup hid in the bushes.

_____ 9. Rebecca and I quarreled.

_____10. We drove to the Pacific Coast.

_____11. We rented a cottage on the beach.

_____12. Margaret arrived at noon.

_____13. Our club meets on Tuesday night.

_____14. I bought a souvenir for the babysitter.

Subject, Verb, and Object (S-V-O)

In the **S-V-O** sentence pattern, a direct object follows the verb. It names the person or thing directly acted on by the action described by the verb. It answers the question *who* or *what* after the action verb. Modifiers (adjectives, adverbs, and prepositional phrases) do not affect the sentence pattern.

Examples:

S	V	DO
Robert	*met*	*Elizabeth.*
Robert	*ate*	*cookies.*
Robert	*knew*	*them.*
Sly Robert	*knew*	*details* of the twisted plot.

Read each sentence. Write SVO if the sentence fits this pattern. Underline the subject once, the verb twice, and circle the direct object. Write *no* if it does not fit the SVO pattern.

_____ 1. Zachary gave the money to Charles.

_____ 2. Ralph sharpened his pencil before class.

_____ 3. The dollar fell under the table.

_____ 4. Ed mowed the grass in the backyard.

_____ 5. Monica concocts her own facial of cucumbers and honey.

_____ 6. Carla found a five dollar bill in the street.

_____ 7. After the battle, most of the enemy surrendered.

_____ 8. Fagin and Bill Sykes kidnapped Oliver Twist in the novel by Dickens.

_____ 9. Mrs. Blanchard frequently called daytime talk shows.

_____10. Benny took his sister's ice cream and ate it.

_____11. Evelyn rests in the afternoon after work.

_____12. Albert burned his hand on the grill of the barbecue pit.

Subject, Verb, Indirect Object, Direct Object (S-V-IO-DO)

In the **S-V-IO-DO** sentence pattern, an indirect object tells *to whom* or *for whom* a direct object is intended. It immediately follows the verb and is followed by the direct object. Modifiers (adjectives, adverbs, and prepositional phrases) do not affect the sentence pattern.

Examples:

S	V	IO	DO
Patty	*gave*	*Sharon*	a *present.*
Patty	*gave*	*her*	a *present.*
Patty	*gave*	young *Sharon*	a *present.*

Read each sentence. Write *yes* in the blank if the sentence fits the S-V-IO-DO pattern. Divide the sentence into subject (S), verb (V), direct object (DO), and indirect object (IO). Write *no*, if the sentence does not fit this pattern. The first one has been done for you.

<u>yes</u>   1. Lee / gave / Dave / a fax machine for Christmas.
          S   V   IO   DO

_____   2. Evelyn told her mother a lie.

_____   3. Martha left her purse in the car.

_____   4. The unscrupulous man sold the elderly couple some worthless land.

_____   5. Her mother sent a birthday box to Meghan at camp.

_____   6. Chris sent her daughter to Europe as a graduation present.

_____   7. Lynette gave the fuzzy puppy a big hug.

_____   8. Mr. Ullrich left Malcolm a big project for the weekend.

_____   9. The tutor gave Steven some much-needed help in math.

_____ 10. Marianna writes to her penpal frequently.

_____ 11. Blake bought his colleague a cup of coffee.

_____ 12. Roger drives his sister to school on Tuesday.

Name _____   Sentence Patterns

Subject, Verb, Direct Object, Object Complement (S-V-DO-OC)

In the **S-V-DO-OC** pattern, a noun or adjective called an **object complement**, identifies or describes the direct object. The object complement follows the direct object.

Examples:

S	V	DO	OC
Alyssa	*found*	the *movie*	*amusing.*
Kim	*named*	her *daughter*	*Allison.*

Read each sentence. Write *yes* in the blank if the sentence fits the S-V-DO-OC pattern. Divide the sentence into subject (S), verb (V), direct object (DO), and object complement (OC). Write *no* if the sentence does not fit this pattern.

_____ 1. The hurricane / made / our sliding glass door / dangerous.
              S   V   DO   OC

_____ 2. Mrs. Bell considered the children foolish.

_____ 3. We saw the president during the White House tour.

_____ 4. The elderly woman was declared incompetent by her heirs.

_____ 5. The deer gave the hunter a good chase.

_____ 6. The judges declared my sister Miss Teenage America.

_____ 7. The critic called the movie a flop.

_____ 8. We painted the trim bright white.

_____ 9. The new interstate entrance makes downtown convenient.

_____10. The neighborhood found the farm animals objectionable.

_____11. The students found the new jazz group very innovative.

_____12. The class elected Marvin treasurer.

_____13. The explanation of iambic pentameter was making Dorothy sleepy.

_____14. Her high blood pressure made her condition worse.

© Carson-Dellosa CD-3745   48

Subject, Linking Verb, and Predicate Adjective (S-LV-PA)

In the **S-LV-PA** pattern, the subject is followed by a linking verb. The linking verb describes conditions, not actions, and connects the subject with adjectives that follow it. In addition to forms of the verb *to be* and *become,* other common linking verbs used in S-LV-PA patterns include *seem, become, appear, look, taste, feel, smell, sound, stay, grow,* and *remain.*

Example: S   LV   PA
                His *date*   *became*   *bored* with the subject.

Read the sentence. Write *yes* if the sentence follows the S-LV-PA pattern. Divide the sentence into subject (S), linking verb (V), and predicate adjective (PA). Write *no* if the sentence does not fit this pattern.

_____ 1. Jane's new watch / looks / expensive.
                        S   V   PA

_____ 2. The house appeared adequate for such a large family.

_____ 3. I found the heat unbearable.

_____ 4. Marie's stomach felt terrible after lunch.

_____ 5. Audrey Hepburn was a very talented actress.

_____ 6. Fred Astaire's dancing was memorable.

_____ 7. Maggie was sad about her grade on the essay.

_____ 8. Willard grew sleepy during the long lecture.

_____ 9. Sally seemed uncomfortable around Matthew.

_____ 10. Ms. Davis is the leader in the polls.

_____ 11. The street was too noisy on the weekends.

_____ 12. The faculty felt hostile towards the inflexible new principal.

Subject, Linking Verb, and Predicate Nominative (S-LV-PN)

In the **S-LV-PN** pattern, the predicate nominative following the linking verb renames the subject. The linking verb describes conditions, not actions. Forms of the verb *to be* (*am, is, are, was,* and *were*) are the most common linking verbs. Another common linking verb used in this sentence pattern is *to become.* Modifiers (adjectives, adverbs, and prepositional
phrases) do not affect the sentence pattern.

Example: <u>S</u>   <u>LV</u>   <u>PN</u>
                 My favorite *snack*   is   chocolate *cake*.

Notice that this sentence can be reversed, so that the predicate nominative becomes the subject and vice versa.

Example: <u>S</u>   <u>LV</u>   <u>PN</u>
                 Chocolate *cake*   is   my favorite *snack*.

Read each sentence. If the pattern is S-LV-PN, write *yes* in the blank and rewrite the sentence so that the PN becomes the subject. If the sentence is not in this pattern, write *no*.

_____ 1. **An orange is a good source of vitamin C.**

           _____

_____ 2. **Computerization is the solution to their antiquated system.**

           _____

_____ 3. **This credit card charges no annual fee.**

           _____

_____ 4. **Julie Andrews is a dearly-beloved singer.**

           _____

_____ 5. **Jody was delighted to find money in her pocket.**

           _____

_____ 6. **The man in the Hawaiian shirt is my doctor.**

           _____

Noun Function in Sentence Patterns

Read the following sentences. Each contains an underlined noun. Determine the function of the noun in each sentence. Decide between subject (S), direct object (DO), object complement (OC), predicate nominative (PN). Write the function in the blank provided.

_____ 1. Louisa May Alcott was the <u>author</u> of *Little Women.*

_____ 2. Alcott wrote many successful <u>novels</u>.

_____ 3. Her spunky <u>heroine</u> Jo is a great favorite with young readers.

_____ 4. Jo's <u>dream</u> was to become a published writer.

_____ 5. Her <u>talent</u> flourished under the guidance of Professor Baer.

_____ 6. Amy was Jo's <u>sister</u>.

_____ 7. Amy destroyed Jo's precious <u>manuscript</u> in retaliation for a sisterly squabble.

_____ 8. This incident made Jo <u>angry</u>.

_____ 9. Jo felt no <u>jealousy</u> toward Amy when Amy eventually married Laurie.

_____10. Jo had the closest <u>relationship</u> with her sister Beth.

_____11. The <u>death</u> of Beth is one of the most poignant episodes in the novel.

_____12. Beth's selfless <u>life</u> contributed to her untimely death.

_____13. Jo had many good <u>times</u> with her older sister Meg.

_____14. Although Jo felt uncomfortable at dances, Meg loved the elegance and <u>gaiety</u>.

Sentence Pattern Review

Read the following sentences. Each contains the noun *sister*. Determine the function of *sister* in each sentence. Label the function as one of the following:

          S—subject   **DO—direct object**
          OC—object complement   **IO—indirect object**
          PN—predicate nominative

_____ 1. Amy March is Meg March's youngest <u>sister</u>.

_____ 2. Mrs. Laurence and Laurie considered each other <u>sisters</u>.

_____ 3. Although Beth survived rheumatic fever, this <u>sister</u> would never regain her health.

_____ 4. Meg gave her <u>sister</u> Amy some money to buy limes.

_____ 5. To everyone's surprise, Laurie married the youngest <u>sister</u> instead of Jo.

_____ 6. Jo is the <u>sister</u> who is definitely the central character.

_____ 7. Aunt March showed obvious partiality to the youngest <u>sister</u>.

_____ 8. Meg was the oldest <u>sister</u> in the March family as well as the prettiest.

_____ 9. The <u>sister</u> most involved in acts of charity was gentle Beth.

_____10. Mr. Laurence gave Beth a piano because he was particularly fond of this <u>sister</u>.

Use the noun *school* in any three of the functions listed above.

1. _____

2. _____

3. _____

Simple Sentence

A **simple sentence** consists of a single independent clause or complete thought. It can have more than one subject, and more than one verb and still be a simple sentence. It can be lengthened by adding modifiers and complements.

Examples:
The vase fell. (one subject, one verb)
The vase and statue fell. (two subjects, one verb)
The vase fell and broke. (one subject, two verbs)
The vase and statue fell and broke. (two subjects, two verbs)
The fragile vase fell off the dresser and completely shattered. (one subject, two verbs, many modifiers)

Write S if the sentence is simple. Write *no* if it is not simple.

_____ 1. Madeleine hungrily ate grapes at the table.

_____ 2. Jack and Elizabeth drank milk out of the carton.

_____ 3. Roger is the distinguished man in the dark blue suit.

_____ 4. Roger, who is a noted inventor, is working on a secret project.

_____ 5. The girl looked in the mirror and combed her pretty hair.

_____ 6. The ghost appears in the hall every night and terrorizes the guests.

_____ 7. Drew yawned and stretched, but he could not get out of bed.

_____ 8. Sharon paints landscapes well.

_____ 9. We all knew who was in trouble.

_____10. The outfielders were missing easy fly balls.

_____11. Gladys was not tired, but her tennis partner was.

_____12. A person who has mastered a second language is bilingual.

Compound Sentences

A **compound sentence** contains two or more independent clauses. The coordinating conjunction (*and, but, so, or, nor,* or *yet*) that joins the two independent clauses suggests that the two clauses are equally important. A comma usually precedes the coordinating conjunction, but may be omitted if the first clause is short. A semicolon can take the place of the coordinating conjunction.

Examples: Most of the girls favored the suggestion, but the boys did not.
                   Most of the girls favored the suggestion; the boys did not.
                   That was fun but now we must go home.

Write CMP if the sentence is compound or *no* if it is not compound.

_____ 1. The weather was perfect, and everyone eagerly anticipated the outing.

_____ 2. The cat chased the mouse which had eluded him for days.

_____ 3. Liza sang ten songs, but the audience clamored for more.

_____ 4. He spotted the horse, but it quickly galloped away.

_____ 5. Glenda played basketball and won a sports scholarship.

_____ 6. A strange dog chased us, but his owner came to our rescue.

_____ 7. Ruby bought the blouse, and the brooch was given to her.

_____ 8. She labeled Jack foolhardy, and she pronounced Jill foolish.

_____ 9. The writer got discouraged when he had been rejected three times.

_____10. I brought cash, but it wasn't enough.

_____11. The airfare was cheap, so Marva bought the ticket.

_____12. *The 60's* by Blake Bailey is informative and entertaining.

Complex Sentences

A **complex sentence** contains one independent clause and one or more dependent clauses. The independent clause is the more important of the two, and the dependent clause modifies it in some way. A clause introduced by a subordinating conjunction can appear within the independent clause as well as before or after it.

Examples: When we saw the repair estimate, we decided to buy a new car.
We didn't think we could afford a new car, until we saw the cost of repairs.
Because the cost of repairs was so high, we bought a new car.
The girl sitting in the front who is driving the red convertible is my sister.

Write CPX if the sentence is complex. Underline the independent clause once and underline the dependent clause(s) twice. Write *no* if the sentence is not complex.

_____ 1. The roof leaks whenever it rains.

_____ 2. I told the ophthalmologist that I was seeing double since I got my new glasses.

_____ 3. Because the city faces a huge deficit, a new tax has been proposed.

_____ 4. Lauren told me that the idea was hers because she thought of it first.

_____ 5. When a player spikes the volleyball, he hits it sharply downward.

_____ 6. Charles is a perfectionist who rarely fails to spot an error.

_____ 7. The nickel has diminished in value since it can no longer buy a telephone call.

_____ 8. The dog barks incessantly whenever the mailman comes.

_____ 9. Venice is accessible by boat or foot, but not by car.

_____10. Avery is one of those kids who always scores high on tests.

_____11. Whenever Vincent thinks of Vanessa who is his girlfriend, he smiles.

_____12. The artist painted lovely Venetian scenes in watercolor.

Compound-Complex Sentences

Compound-Complex sentences combine two (or more) independent clauses and at least one dependent clause.

Example: Mark tried to do the algebra homework alone, but he realized that he needed some assistance after he had spent several hours on it.

Write CC if the sentence is compound-complex. Underline the independent clauses once. Underline the dependent clause(s) twice. Write *no* if the sentence is not compound-complex.

_____ 1. We use whatever is donated, but we especially welcome toys.

_____ 2. The room that Carrie painted had been white, but she changed the color to pale blue.

_____ 3. You are the person who I want to see.

_____ 4. She was going to the beach for the weekend until the tropical storm developed, so she decided to change her plans.

_____ 5. The masker who had worn the striking jester costume was in the contest, but he did not win first prize.

_____ 6. Although Bill was hesitant to run for mayor, his friends encouraged him, and he entered the race.

_____ 7. What kind of car do you want to buy?

_____ 8. While Valerie was shopping for souvenirs, Michael was snorkeling at the reef, and Monica was taking a guided tour of the island.

_____ 9. Colonel Mowry was reading in the study, and Professor Peach was napping in the conservatory, when the murder took place.

_____10. The wine was superb and the food was excellent although the service was definitely lacking.

Review

Rewrite each sentence as directed in the parentheses that follow it. S is simple, CD is compound, CX is complex, and CC is compound-complex.

Example: The dog was barking incessantly, and the cat was crying loudly. (CD to CC)
            <u>When the thunderstorm reached its peak, the dog was barking incessantly</u>
            <u>and</u> the cat was crying loudly.

1. **Just as the plane departed, the passenger arrived at the airport. (CX to CC)**

    _____

    _____

2. **The carpet was ruined in the flood, and the chairs were damaged. (CD to CX)**

    _____

    _____

3. **The electricity went out during the storm. (S to CD)**

    _____

    _____

4. **The fax machine ran out of paper. (S to CX)**

    _____

    _____

5. **There was broken glass everywhere, and I didn't have a broom. (CD to CC)**

    _____

    _____

6. **After I let the cake cool, I iced it with fudge frosting. (CX to CD)**

    _____

    _____

Review

Classify each of the following sentences as one of the following:

S) Simple   **CD)** Compound   **CX)** Complex   **CC)** Compound Complex

_____ 1. If you do not help me, I will fail the course.

_____ 2. I have investigated the new building project thoroughly.

_____ 3. Marcia lives in Houston, but her brother John lives here.

_____ 4. Since we have begun this discussion, you have refused to listen.

_____ 5. If he changes his mind, order him to leave.

_____ 6. A woman, who was wearing a big hat, sat in front of me at the movies.

_____ 7. Sue lectured the first hour, and we asked questions the second hour.

_____ 8. My brother is good at water skiing, but he is a dunce at snow skiing.

_____ 9. Although you are a friend, I must disapprove of your actions.

_____10. Margaret refused because she had other plans.

_____11. Everyone always laughs when Arthur sneezes.

_____12. Diana waited patiently, but the bus never came.

_____13. I am sure that James does not know what danger is involved, and he will get in trouble.

_____14. Behind the church was a path that led to the cemetery.

_____15. The telephone rang twice, and Stevie, who was closest, answered it.

_____16. Uncle Elton arrived after everyone had gone to bed.

Review

Classify each of the following sentences as one of the following:

S) Simple   **CD**) Compound   **CX**) Complex   **CC**) Compound Complex

_____ 1. Matt can do a triple flip, and Kathy can do a double flip.

_____ 2. Since I joined the speech club, I have had more self-confidence.

_____ 3. Jim Thomas, who lives next door, is going to camp in July.

_____ 4. The spokes are broken, and the frame is rusty and bent.

_____ 5. If you want to arrive on time, listen carefully to the directions.

_____ 6. Flights to Dallas, Los Angeles, and San Francisco leave in ten minutes.

_____ 7. I need a major overhaul on my bicycle.

_____ 8. Dad washes the dishes, and Mom mows the lawn.

_____ 9. My mother was wrong this time, and I told her that I did not agree.

_____10. I think that I am the smartest kid around.

_____11. Anyone who is a member may bring a guest.

_____12. Sara enjoys the company of small children.

_____13. We all knew the one who had received top honors in math.

_____14. Cypress was first settled by the Greeks.

_____15. You must abide by the rules of the contract, or you will lose your job.

_____16. Louise is the best biologist in the laboratory.

_____17. Because we were so late, we called a taxi.

_____18. Mark read the story and laughed to himself.

Gerunds

A **gerund** is a verb form used as a noun. It uses the *-ing* verb ending. Like verbs, gerunds name actions or conditions. Like nouns, gerunds function in sentences as subjects (**S**), direct objects (**DO**), predicate nominatives (**PN**), or objects of prepositions (**OP**). A gerund can stand alone, or it can be part of a gerund phrase.

Examples: Dame Van Winkle's <u>nagging</u> made Rip's life miserable. (gerund as **S**)
Rip Van Winkle hated his wife's <u>nagging</u>. (gerund as **DO**)
The cause of Rip's discontent was his wife's <u>nagging</u>. (gerund as **PN**)
Rip's life from the constant <u>nagging</u> was unbearable. (gerund as **OP**)

Underline the gerund in each of the following sentences.

1. **The driver was fined for littering on the highway.**

2. **He found running for office to be a grueling experience.**

3. **Smoking was ruining his health.**

4. **Reading was a challenging activity to the six year old.**

5. **Eating homemade ice cream was the ruination of her diet.**

6. **Packing for summer camp took Meghan all weekend.**

Underline the gerund. Classify its function in the sentence from the following: S, DO, PN, or OP. If there is no gerund in the sentence, write NONE.

_____ 1. **Playing tennis is great aerobic exercise.**

_____ 2. **The teacher loved singing as a way to unwind.**

_____ 3. **The object of the game was winning.**

_____ 4. **He bought those new shoes for golfing .**

_____ 5. **Marrying him is her goal.**

Participles

A **participle** is a verb form used as an adjective.

Examples: Drew had a flat-bottomed <u>fishing</u> boat.
                    I sat in the <u>broken</u> chair.

Look at the underlined word in each sentence. Write V if the under-lined word functions as a verb. Write P if it functions as a participle (verbal).

_____ 1. My former English teacher is <u>running</u> for public office.

_____ 2. I forgot my <u>running</u> shoes.

_____ 3. The <u>dented</u> fender was an unpleasant surprise.

_____ 4. Someone just <u>dented</u> the bumper of my car.

_____ 5. My neighbors will soon be <u>moving</u>.

_____ 6. They'll need to rent a <u>moving</u> van.

_____ 7. The <u>misplaced</u> memo caused big problems.

_____ 8. Whom do you think <u>misplaced</u> the memo?

_____ 9. I hope that I have an <u>experienced</u> pilot on this flight.

_____10. I <u>experienced</u> air sickness from the turbulence.

_____11. Molly was surprised to learn that an oyster is a <u>living</u> creature.

_____12. The <u>living</u> conditions in the tenement were not acceptable.

_____13. Carmen is <u>chilling</u> the champagne.

_____14. A <u>chilling</u> tale was told around the campfire.

_____15. The <u>proposed</u> amendment was very controversial.

Name _____ **Verbals**

Gerund and Participle Review

**Look at each underlined word. Classify it as one of the following:
gerund (G), participle (P), or verb (V).**

_____ 1. The detective is <u>investigating</u> a domestic matter.

_____ 2. The <u>investigating</u> officer was called to the stand.

_____ 3. By <u>investigating</u>, I was able to find the answer.

_____ 4. Morton especially loves <u>skiing</u> in Bornio.

_____ 5. The advanced students are <u>skiing</u> on a different slope.

_____ 6. The <u>skiing</u> instructor was from Utah.

_____ 7. <u>Participating</u> in the dangerous rescue attempt was heroic.

_____ 8. All of the local high schools are <u>participating</u> in the speech tournament.

_____ 9. Get your free gift at all <u>participating</u> stores.

_____10. Claudia enjoys <u>volunteering</u> at Children's Hospital.

_____11. Jana is <u>volunteering</u> her time at a homeless shelter.

_____12. Are you <u>volunteering</u> to help?

_____13. Anis is <u>reading</u> a new Stephen King novel.

_____14. Mrs. Cunningham is her <u>reading</u> teacher.

_____15. Roxanna enjoys <u>reading</u> more than any other activity.

_____16. <u>Flying</u> to Hong Kong is very expensive.

_____17. I am <u>flying</u> to Hong Kong in November.

_____18. Carlo took <u>flying</u> lessons when he was twenty.

Name _____   **Verbals**

Infinitives as Nouns

Infinitives are verb forms preceded by the word *to*. They can be used in sentences as nouns, adjectives, or adverbs. When **infinitives function as nouns**, they can be used as subjects (**S**), predicate nominatives (**PN**), direct objects (**DO**), or objects of prepositions (**OP**).

Examples: My choice is <u>to leave</u>. (infinitive as PN)
<u>To redesign</u> would take a long time. (infinitive as S)
The child began <u>to cry</u> . (infinitive as DO)
She did not respond except <u>to glare</u>. (infinitive as OP)
I gave a hug to my friend. (no infinitive)

Underline the infinitive in each sentence. Then write S if it is used as a subject, DO if it is used as a direct object, PN if it is used as a predicate nominative, or OP if the infinitive is used as an object of a preposition. If there is no infinitive, write NONE.

_____ 1. I just want to finish.

_____ 2. Her passion is to dance.

_____ 3. To walk is good exercise.

_____ 4. I will walk to the mall.

_____ 5. My penmanship needs to improve.

_____ 6. Our maid refuses to iron.

_____ 7. I gave a pass to Patrick.

_____ 8. To escape was impossible.

_____ 9. To believe is very difficult in this instance.

_____10. He has nothing on his mind right now except to sleep.

_____11. I want to look, but it's too scary.

_____12. To win is our goal.

© Carson Dellosa CD-3745   63

Infinitives as Adjectives and Adverbs

An infinitive may be used as an adjective when it directly modifies a noun or pronoun in a sentence. It may also be used as an adverb when it directly modifies a verb, adjective, or adverb in the sentence.

Examples: Clara likes chocolate milk <u>to drink</u>. (infinitive as adjective)
                  They were disappointed <u>to leave</u>. (infinitive as adverb)

Underline the infinitive in each sentence. Classify it as one of the following: (ADJ) adjective or (ADV) adverb.

_____ 1. She is a person to admire.

_____ 2. This watch is the best one to buy.

_____ 3. I have a train to catch.

_____ 4. Molly was too frightened to move.

_____ 5. Ms. Jacobs plays golf to relax.

_____ 6. Kathleen was too tired to study.

_____ 7. He has a hard face to forget.

_____ 8. I have promises to keep.

_____ 9. This map is hard to read.

_____10. The name of that country is difficult to spell.

_____11. This map is easy to read.

_____12. The kitten's fur was so soft to touch.

_____13. That malicious comment will be hard to forgive.

_____14. This math textbook is designed to provide constant review.

_____15. A driver who has had many accidents is difficult to insure.

Infinitive Phrases as Adjectives and Adverbs

An **infinitive phrase** contains an infinitive and any other words (subjects, objects, and modifiers) needed to complete its meaning. **Infinitive phrases** can function as nouns, adjectives, and adverbs in addition to functioning as nouns.

Examples: The counselor told Mrs. Martin that *Reviving Ophelia* was a good
                    book <u>to read from cover to cover</u>. (adjective phrase)

                    Sam approached the teacher <u>to explain the situation</u>. (adverb phrase)

Underline each infinitive phrase. Identify it as adjective (ADJ) or adverb (ADV).

_____ 1. **Your address is easy to remember at any time.**

_____ 2. **Models use make-up tricks to cover flaws in their appearances.**

_____ 3. **The best type of cheese to eat with a red pasta sauce is Romano.**

_____ 4. **Meghan mostly uses her computer to type essays.**

_____ 5. **Alyssa has never been the type to gossip about other students.**

_____ 6. **The best time to go to Disney World is in the fall.**

_____ 7. **Babysitting is a good way to learn responsibility.**

_____ 8. **I need a screwdriver to take apart this bookcase.**

_____ 9. **Brian had a lot of money to spend at the sporting goods store.**

_____10. **Sylvia was the best singer to audition for the part.**

_____11. **The commander gave orders to bomb the target.**

_____12. **To prepare for the test, Anthony needs quiet.**

Name _____   **Verbals**

Infinitives as Noun Phrases

An **infinitive phrase** is a group of words consisting of an infinitive and any other words (subjects, objects, and modifiers) needed to complete its meaning. Infinitive phrases can function as a subjects (**S**), predicate nominatives (**PN**), direct objects (**DO**), or objects of prepositions (**OP**).

Examples: Amy wants <u>to find a new job</u>. (infinitive phrase as DO)
<u>To skate in The Olympics</u> is her dream. (infinitive phrase as S)
Her dream is <u>to skate in the Olympics</u>. (infinitive phrase as PN)
I gave a lecture <u>to the defiant young offender</u>. (no infinitive phrase)

Underline each infinitive phrase and identify it as a subject (S), direct object (DO), or predicate nominative (PN). Write *no* if the sentence contains no infinitive phrase.

_____ 1. Mary loves to eat tomatoes from her own garden.

_____ 2. To dance at Radio City Music Hall is her fantasy.

_____ 3. Valerie wants to finish college in four years.

_____ 4. To finish this project quickly would be a blessing.

_____ 5. Mrs. Shaw just wanted to feel better.

_____ 6. We are about to see a new invention.

_____ 7. To read this entire novel is my weekend homework.

_____ 8. I gave a copy to my cousin Elizabeth.

_____ 9. I tried to stop her, but I failed.

_____10. Does anyone plan to attend the Fourth of July picnic?

_____11. To follow his lead would be a major mistake.

_____12. Mrs. Matherne's dream is to own her own business.

Split Infinitives

When a word, phrase, or clause comes between the infinitive *to* and the verb that follows, it is called a **split infinitive**. This generally results in an awkward sentence. Although there are a few exceptions, it is best to move the word or words that split the infinitive to the end of the sentence or some other spot.

Examples: A reliable car does not need to necessarily be expensive. (awkward)
                A reliable car does not necessarily need to be expensive. (better)

Read each sentence. Underline the infinitive. Rewrite the sentence so that there is not a split infinitive.

1. **The new movie was designed to directly appeal to preteen girls.**

   _____

   _____

2. **The child liked to immediately tattle when the opportunity arose.**

   _____

   _____

3. **The talkative couple in the theater was asked to finally stop.**

   _____

   _____

4. **Beth decided to more neatly rewrite her essay.**

   _____

   _____

5. **Everyone was told to as soon as possible vacate the premises.**

   _____

   _____

Clauses

Independent and Subordinate Clauses

An **independent (or main) clause** contains a subject and a verb and can stand alone as a sentence. A **subordinate (or dependent) clause** contains a subject and verb, but cannot stand alone as a sentence. The subordinate clause clarifies or adds to the meaning of the independent clause that it accompanies.

Examples: <u>If you need help with your homework</u>, I will help you.
The dress <u>that you chose</u> is too expensive.
(The subordinate clauses are underlined.)

Complete each sentence below by adding a subordinate clause or independent clause. In the blank write IND (independent) or SUB (subordinate) to identify the type of clause you wrote.

_____ 1. _____, you can't borrow the car.

_____ 2. **If you feed that cat,** _____.

_____ 3. **The girl** _____ **is my brother's girlfriend.**

_____ 4. _____, **Mark got an A on the exam.**

_____ 5. _____ **who was chosen to be Miss America.**

_____ 6. **Since I couldn't find you,** _____.

_____ 7. **I visited an island** _____.

_____ 8. _____, **I can't go with you.**

_____ 9. _____, **I'll be home early.**

_____ 10. **If Henry shows up,** _____.

Independent and Dependent Clauses

Identify each clause as independent (IN) or dependent (D). Underline the subordinating conjunction or relative pronoun if there is one. No punctuation or capitalization is provided.

_____ 1. she wears too much makeup

_____ 2. since she is under a lot of stress

_____ 3. until the entire project is complete

_____ 4. we were thirty minutes late for the appointment

_____ 5. because you're afraid

_____ 6. they felt more comfortable with me

_____ 7. if the turkey is not refrigerated

_____ 8. although the report was in plain view

_____ 9. which is in demand

_____10. who knows my brother

_____11. shadows are longer in the winter

_____12. it is homemade

_____13. when the plant is over watered

_____14. it was raining

_____15. because good records were not kept

_____16. until the light bulb was invented

_____17. that I wear to church

_____18. Sal is arachnophobic

Independent and Subordinate Clauses

An **independent clause** can stand alone as a sentence. A **subordinate or dependent clause** contains a subject and verb, but does not express a complete thought and can't stand alone as a sentence. The subordinate clause must be attached to the independent clause to complete the meaning. Subordinate clauses are begun with a subordinating conjunction such as *although, because, if, since, until,* and *when* or relative pronouns such as *who, which,* and *that.*

Identify each clause as independent (IND) or subordinate (SUB).

_____ 1. although the cookies were low in fat

_____ 2. they were still high in calories

_____ 3. Jack paid all his bills

_____ 4. after he received a second notice

_____ 5. who wants seats in the first balcony

_____ 6. the people must buy their tickets months in advance

_____ 7. Mr. Stickney used his car phone to call a tow truck

_____ 8. after his car overheated

_____ 9. the icemaker is broken

_____10. although the refrigerator is new

_____11. Marcia wears high heels every day

_____12. since she works downtown

_____13. until the road construction is completed

_____14. we have to leave thirty minutes earlier

_____15. since you don't have a flashlight

Adjective Clauses

Adjective clauses modify a noun or pronoun in the independent clause and are introduced by *who, which*, or *that*.

Example: The coach <u>who was hired last week</u> is doing an impressive job.

Complete each sentence with an adjective clause.

1. The woman _____ is a famous French chef.

2. The person _____ was wearing a white uniform.

3. The rumor _____ is totally untrue.

4. The family _____ is from Costa Rica.

5. He is the thief _____.

6. The purse _____ was an expensive Italian designer bag.

7. The diamond brooch _____ was a fake.

8. The book _____ was unsuitable for the young children.

9. The seamstress _____ did not follow the pattern as directed.

10. I read an advertisement _____.

Adjective Clauses

An **adjective clause** is a subordinate clause that modifies a noun or pronoun in the independent (or main) clause. The adjective clause is usually introduced by a relative pronoun such as *who, which,* or *that* and comes right after the word it modifies.

Example: The skirt <u>which is part of my school uniform</u> is blue and green plaid.

Underline the adjective clause once. Underline the relative pronoun twice. Write the word that it modifies in the blank.

_____ 1. The man who sat at the next table in the restaurant was smoking in the non-smoking section.

_____ 2. The students who did not do their homework got a detention.

_____ 3. I broke the crystal perfume bottle that sat on my dresser.

_____ 4. The educational systems that are currently in Europe, Asia, Africa, and South America are quite dissimilar to those in North America.

_____ 5. The civilization that spoke Latin began to disappear after the collapse of the Roman Empire in 476 A.D.

_____ 6. The modern languages which eventually replaced Latin include French, Spanish, Italian, Rumanian, and Portuguese.

_____ 7. Probably one of the most important contributions that the Romans left behind was their language.

_____ 8. Did you take the black pen that I was using?

_____ 9. The person who took my pen got away with a very expensive writing instrument.

_____10. It is the pen that I got for a graduation present.

72

Restrictive and Nonrestrictive Clauses

Adjective clauses can be restrictive or nonrestrictive. **Restrictive clauses** are essential to identifying a noun or pronoun, and they are not set apart by commas. **Nonrestrictive** clauses provide additional information about the noun or pronoun, but are not essential to specific identification. Nonrestrictive clauses are enclosed in commas.

Examples: The dress that Camilla wears to the theater is a simple black sheath. (restrictive)
Camilla's favorite dress, which she often wears to the theater, is a simple black sheath. (nonrestrictive)

Underline the adjective clause. Write RES if it is restrictive, and NRS if it is nonrestrictive. If there is no adjective clause, write NONE.

_____ 1. **Baton Rouge, which is the capital of Louisiana, is in the heart of Cajun country.**

_____ 2. **When we are driving through Baton Rouge, we stop for delicious Cajun food.**

_____ 3. **A city which is noted for good Cajun food is Baton Rouge.**

_____ 4. **Tricycles, which are beginner bicycles, have three wheels.**

_____ 5. **Bicycles that have three wheels are called tricycles.**

_____ 6. **The man who is squinting is the lifeguard.**

_____ 7. **Since the lifeguard has a large expanse of beach to watch, he must be very alert.**

_____ 8. **The lifeguard, who happens to be my sister's boyfriend, was late for duty.**

_____ 9. **Espresso, which is my favorite drink, is very strong.**

_____ 10. **Coffee that is grown in Colombia tastes best to me.**

Adverb Clauses

An **adverb clause** is a subordinate clause that functions as an adverb to modify the independent clause. Adverb clauses answer the question *when, how, where,* or *why*. They are introduced by a subordinating conjunction. Common subordinating conjunctions include *after, as, before, once, until, when, whenever, while, as if, as though, if, unless, whether, although, though, how, where, wherever, because, whereas,* and *since*.

Examples: <u>After we finish studying</u>, I'll order pizza. (when)
Alex answered the question <u>as if he were well-prepared</u>. (how)
<u>Wherever you go</u>, I'll find you. (where)
I failed <u>because I didn't study</u>. (why)

Underline the adverb clause in each sentence once. Underline the subordinating conjunction twice. Leave the sentence blank if there is no adverb clause.

1. The cookies taste great because they were made from scratch.

2. If chicken is not properly washed, harmful bacteria may be consumed.

3. After their first date, Marcelo and Anna became good friends.

4. Although she worked almost every night, Valerie was a full-time student.

5. Margaret read an interesting article while she sat on the bus.

6. Mrs. Garland couldn't drive home since she lost her only key.

7. I'll fix your glasses while you wait.

8. When the daffodils bloom, spring is here.

9. Wherever I go, my little brother tags along.

10. Although alligators look very much like crocodiles, they are usually not as dangerous.

Adverb Clauses

An **adverb clause** is a subordinate clause that functions as an adverb to modify the independent clause. It is usually introduced by a subordinating conjunction.

Example: <u>Because the road had become so slick during the rainstorm</u>, Ms. Harris decided to postpone the field trip.

Complete each sentence below by adding an adverb clause.

1. _____, all of the dogs in the neighborhood bark.

2. _____, I was surprised to see a barn owl.

3. _____, we could see an eleventh century Rhine castle.

4. We spent the night in the German medieval town of Rothenburg der Tauber

   _____.

5. _____, we looked it up in the dictionary.

6. We were all skeptical, _____.

7. _____, Jane bought her a pretty set of goblets.

8. _____, Jean almost got hit by the arrow.

9. Brandon could see the face of the clock in the darkness

   _____.

10. _____, Elizabeth found the water fountain too unsanitary to use.

Noun Clauses

Subordinate clauses that function as nouns are called **noun clauses**. They can function in a sentence as a subject, direct object, predicate nominative, object of preposition, or anywhere that you find a simple noun.

Examples: <u>What he told me</u> was very cruel. (noun clause as subject)
I gave <u>whatever I could spare</u> to the homeless man.
(noun clause as direct object)
Our study group will be <u>whoever shows up</u>.
(noun clause as predicate nominative)
Mr. Phipps gives help after school to <u>whoever needs it</u>.
(noun clause as object of the preposition)

**Underline the noun clause in each sentence. Write its function:
S for subject, DO for direct object, PN for predicate nominative, or OP for object of the preposition.**

_____ 1. **Please tell me who painted this landscape.**

_____ 2. **My concern is that I won't have enough time.**

_____ 3. **Why you are dating him is a mystery to me.**

_____ 4. **He bought what he needed at the sporting goods store.**

_____ 5. **I can't believe what you did.**

_____ 6. **Betty talks to whoever will listen.**

_____ 7. **Whoever is responsible for this should step forward.**

_____ 8. **The couch potatoes watched whatever was on television.**

_____ 9. **The homecoming queen will be whoever is most popular.**

_____10. **Whoever lives to the age of one hundred is called a centenarian.**

_____11. **You can do whatever you want.**

_____12. **I will agree with whatever you decide.**

Review

Underline the clause in each sentence and decide which type of clause it is:

    ADJ) Adjective Clause   ADV) Adverb Clause
    N) Noun Clause   NONE) No subordinate Clause

_____ 1. In science class we learned that chalk is made of mostly calcium carbonate.

_____ 2. Advertisements encourage people to want products, and many people cannot distinguish between their wants and their needs.

_____ 3. Liliuokani, who was the last queen of Hawaii, was an accomplished songwriter.

_____ 4. In accordance with school regulations, the school van may be driven by whomever is authorized by the principal.

_____ 5. When Pete lost his fortune, he found himself without friends.

_____ 6. Woodrow Wilson was a Virginian, a democrat, and the 28th President of the United States.

_____ 7. The Indians who inhabited the area of Connecticut around the Naugatuck River were called the Pequots.

_____ 8. I wrote that poem when I was in a whimsical mood.

_____ 9. The beautiful day was rudely interrupted by a tornado.

_____ 10. On the shelf are the three bisque dolls that I recently bought.

_____ 11. Through their popular songs, Ella Fitzgerald, Lena Horne, and Leslie Uggams, who are all contemporary black vocalists, have enriched American music.

_____ 12. The Great Wall of China, which is over 1500 miles long, was built to separate China from Mongolia.

Identifying Phrases

Phrases are combinations of words that go together because they express a single idea. Unlike sentences and clauses, phrases do not contain both a subject and predicate.

Examples: The pretty, young woman caught his eye. (noun phrase)
              I will be attending the coronation. (verb phrase)
              He is married to a movie star. (prepositional phrase)

Look at each underlined phrase. Write in the blank if it is a noun phrase (NP), verb phrase (VP), adjective phrase (ADJP), adverb phrase (ADVP), or prepositional phrase (PP).

_____ 1. Mary Beth was surprised when she couldn't get underline breakfast at Tiffany's.

_____ 2. I am going on condition that my expenses are paid.

_____ 3. The band that will be performing is an old favorite of mine.

_____ 4. She caught a fish with blue gills.

_____ 5. The seagulls soared over the dock.

_____ 6. The mask with warts is really ugly.

_____ 7. I was very amused by the pompous, old gentleman.

_____ 8. He has been trying to meet the pretty tenant in 2C for months.

_____ 9. The boss was thrilled at their work.

_____10. The guests arrived late at night.

_____11. The manager with the paychecks just left.

_____12. The long, meandering path took all afternoon.

Name _____   Sentence Review

Challenge

1. **Determine the pattern in each sentence.**
2. **Identify the type of verbal or verbal phrase.**
3. **Determine if the verbal (or verbal phrase) is used as a noun (functioning as subject, direct object, predicate nominative, object of the preposition), an adjective, or adverb.**

Pattern	Verbal	Function of Verbal
S-V	Gerund (Phrase)	Noun (S, DO, PN, OP)
S-V-DO	Participle (Phrase)	Adjective
S-V-DO-OC	Infinitive (Phrase)	Adverb
S-V-IO-DO		
S-LV-PN		
S-LV-PA		

1. <u>To ride in a gondola</u> is a thrill for children.

   Pattern: _____ Verbal: _____ Function: _____

2. <u>Singing to the tourists</u> earned big tips for the gondola drivers.

   Pattern: _____ Verbal: _____ Function: _____

3. Barbara wants <u>to give</u> her mother a book.

   Pattern: _____ Verbal: _____ Function: _____

4. <u>Following a crooked little street</u> brought Barbara to a shop selling lovely Venetian glass.

   Pattern: _____ Verbal: _____ Function: _____

5. She bought a necklace and <u>matching</u> bracelet from a famous Murano glass factory.

   Pattern: _____ Verbal: _____ Function: _____

6. Barbara's favorite dish <u>to eat</u> in Venice is spaghetti with clams.

   Pattern: _____ Verbal: _____ Function: _____

© Carson Dellosa CD-3745   79

Challenge

1. **Determine the sentence pattern of the independent clause in each sentence.**
2. **Identify the tense of the underlined verb.**
3. **Determine the type of subordinate clause.**

Pattern		Tense		Clause
S-V	Simple Present	Present Progressive		Adjective
S-V-DO	Simple Past	Past Progressive		Adverb
S-V-DO-OC	Simple Future	Future Progressive		Noun
S-V-IO-DO	Present Perfect	Present Perfect Progressive.		
S-LV-PN	Past Perfect	Past Perfect Progressive.		
S-LV-PA	Future Perfect	Future Perfect Progressive.		

1. **After settling in her hotel, Barbara <u>will be heading</u> for her favorite museum.**

   Pattern: _____ Tense: _____ Clause: _____

2. **This art museum, which is called the Galleria degli Uffizi, <u>has been attracting</u> millions of people from all over the world for many years.**

   Pattern: _____ Tense: _____ Clause: _____

3. **Barbara, who is an art history student, <u>will spend</u> several days in the Uffizi.**

   Pattern: _____ Tense: _____ Clause: _____

4. **As tourists were meandering through the halls of the Uffizi, Barbara <u>was observing</u> their reactions to different artists.**

   Pattern: _____ Tense: _____ Clause: _____

5. **Whoever saw the paintings of Botticelli <u>seemed</u> mesmerized.**

   Pattern: _____ Tense: _____ Clause: _____

6. **Pallas and the Centaur, which was painted by Botticelli in 1485, <u>was collecting</u> a large crowd of admirers.**

   Pattern: _____ Tense: _____ Clause: _____

Challenge

1. **Determine the sentence structure in each sentence.**
2. **Look at the underlined noun and identify its function in the sentence.**
3. **Determine if the noun appears in an independent clause or subordinate clause.**

Structure	Function	Clause
Simple (S)	Subject (Sub)	Independent (IND)
Compound (CD)	Direct Object (DO)	Subordinate (SUB)
Complex (CX)	Indirect Object (IO)	
Compound/Complex (CC)	Predicate Nominative (PN)	
	Object of the Preposition (OP)	

1. **She particularly loves the Palantine Hill where the <u>ruins</u> of the palaces of Augustus, Nero, Caracalla, and Tiberius are located.**

   Structure: _____ Function: _____ Clause: _____

2. **Barbara walked from the Palantine Hills to the <u>valley</u> of the Roman Forum.**

   Structure: _____ Function: _____ Clause: _____

3. **She observed the <u>Tempio di Vesta</u> where the goddess's flame was kept burning by the Vestal Virgins.**

   Structure: _____ Function: _____ Clause: _____

4. **The Arco di Tito at the end of the <u>expanse</u> of the forum was built in A.D. 81.**

   Structure: _____ Function: _____ Clause: _____

5. **Barbara noted that the <u>atmosphere</u> of antiquity on the Palantine Hill enchanted Byron when he wrote *Childe Harold*.**

   Structure: _____ Function: _____ Clause: _____

6. **Another site that Barbara found intriguing was the Coliseum, and she spent hours at this place where Christians were literally thrown to the <u>lions</u>.**

   Structure: _____ Function: _____ Clause: _____

Challenge

Follow the directions given to create a sentence.

1. Write an S-V-DO sentence which has the participle form of the verb *to break* describing the direct object.

   _____

   _____

2. Write an S-V-IO-DO sentence which uses the noun *gift* as the direct object.

   _____

   _____

3. Write a complex sentence containing the infinitive form of the verb *to discourage* as the subject of the main clause.

   _____

   _____

4. Write a sentence using a direct quotation which contains the past perfect form of the verb *to run*.

   _____

   _____

5. Write a compound-complex sentence using the noun *book* as the object of a preposition in a subordinate clause.

   _____

   _____

Challenge

Follow the directions given to create a sentence.

1. Write an S-LV-PN sentence using an infinitive or infinitive phrase using the verb *to miss*.

   _____

   _____

2. Write a compound-complex sentence using the verb *to run* in the simple past tense in a subordinate clause.

   _____

   _____

3. Write an S-LV-PA sentence which contains a demonstrative adjective to describe the subject.

   _____

   _____

4. Write an S-V-DO sentence with a gerund or gerund phrase using the verb *to read* as the direct object.

   _____

   _____

5. Write a compound sentence in which the verb in both clauses is a future progressive form of the verb *to go*.

   _____

   _____

Sentence Combining

The following paragraph contains simple sentences with almost no variety in the sentence patterns. Rewrite the paragraph, making sure to include all information, but combining the sentences in ways that make the paragraph more interesting and less choppy.

The Conciergerie is on the Cité in the heart of Paris. It includes three superb Gothic towers. The tour is of great historic interest. You enter through the Guardroom. It has stout pillars with carved capitals. The pillars support the Gothic vaulting. You then enter the Prisoner's Gallery. Here the prisoners had their hands roped behind their backs. Their collars were ripped wide open. Their hair was cut from the nape of their necks before walking into the clerk of court's yard. Next you see Marie Antoinette's prison. She existed in this cell from August 2, 1793 until October 16, 1793. Finally, you see a pathetic patch of grass and a tree. This is the Women's Courtyard. Twelve prisoners were selected daily for the guillotine. They said their farewells here.

_____

_____

_____

_____

_____

_____

_____

_____

_____

Sentence Combining

The following paragraph contains simple sentences with almost no variety in the sentence patterns. Rewrite the paragraph, making sure to include all information, but combining the sentences in ways that make the paragraph more interesting and less choppy.

La Boheme is one of the world's most beloved operas. It was written by Giacomo Puccini. It is based on a novel by Henri Murger. It is written in Italian. It was first performed in 1896 in Turin, Italy. It is set in the Latin Quarter of Paris. The time is about 1830. Act I opens in the attic studio of four struggling, but spirited young men. The male lead is Rudolpho. He is a writer. He meets a young seamstress named Mimi. They fall in love immediately. The lovers go through good times and hard times. Then Mimi becomes very ill. She leaves Rudolpho. In Act IV Mimi returns. She is dying. Rudolpho's friends try to help her. It is too late. Mimi has just come back to see Rudolpho once more. The opera ends with her death. Rudolpho anguishes in sadness and disbelief.

_____

_____

_____

_____

_____

_____

_____

_____

Transformations

Read each sentence. Make all transformations requested.

Example: The artist painted his mother a masterpiece.

         1. Change to a question in the present perfect tense.
           <u>Has the artist painted a masterpiece?</u>

1. **We elected John class president.**

   Change to a question in the future progressive tense.

   _____

   Change to passive voice in the simple past.

   _____

   Change to S-V-O in the present perfect.

   _____

2. **The shy girl became a bold leader.**

   Change to a question in the simple future tense.

   _____

   Change to S-LV-PA in the present progressive tense.

   _____

3. **The directions are easy and the task is easy.**

   Change to a negative statement in the present perfect tense.

   _____

   Change to a simple sentence with a compound subject.

   _____

Sentence Building

Write a sentence using the specific parts of speech requested in the exact order requested.

Example: noun + auxiliary + verb + preposition + article + adjective + noun. (7 words)
            <u>People are flocking to the new restaurant.</u>

1. **Demonstrative pronoun + linking verb + adjective + predicate adjective. (4 words)**

   _____

2. **Concrete noun + conjunction + concrete noun + verb + adverb. (5 words)**

   _____

3. **Collective noun + auxiliary verb + verb + preposition + adjective + noun. (6 words)**

   _____

4. **Article + adjective + noun + adverb + verb + noun. (6 words)**

   _____

5. **Personal pronoun + linking verb + article + compound noun. (4 words)**

   _____

6. **Indefinite pronoun + verb + infinitive. (4 words)**

   _____

7. **Possessive noun + noun + adverb + verb. (4 words)**

   _____

8. **Abstract noun + linking verb + article + adjective + abstract noun. (5 words)**

   _____

9. **Gerund + linking verb + article + adjective + noun. (5 words)**

   _____

10. **Participle + noun + linking verb + predicate adjective. (4 words)**

   _____

A lot and Allot

The phrase **a lot** means "to a considerable quantity or extent." It is never spelled *alot*. The verb **allot** means "to give or assign." Don't confuse these spellings and meanings.

Example: He brought <u>a lot</u> of money.
            Our club <u>allots</u> twenty percent of the proceeds from fundraising to local charities.

Use the correct form of *a lot* or *allot* in each sentence that follows.

1. Thanks _____ for your generous donation to our school fundraising effort.

2. We don't have _____ of money left after receiving that outrageous bill.

3. The Websters decided to _____ $50.00 per paycheck to their vacation fund.

4. I have _____ of homework in math and social studies to do before bed.

5. Meghan _____ a portion of her allowance each week to save for Christmas gifts for her family.

6. There was _____ of blaring music coming from the apartment above ours.

7. Marjorie knows _____ about caring for perennials, but she isn't as knowledgeable about annuals.

8. The school couldn't afford to _____ money from the general fund to the new project.

9. Patrick thought that he had _____ of time to research the topic and write the essay.

10. The Browns _____ ten percent of their income to church donations.

Affect and Effect

Affect means "to act upon, assume, or influence" when used as a verb, and **effect** means "to produce or accomplish."

Example: Your study habits <u>affect</u> your grade. (influence)
                     Your good study habits should <u>effect</u> improvement in your grade. (produce)

Read each sentence carefully to determine if a form of *affect* or *effect* is needed. Write your answer on the line.

1. The movie last night _____ me very much.

2. The book _____ my thinking on the subject of weapons.

3. When she is with that crowd, Melissa _____ an arrogant manner.

4. The board must _____ immediate personnel cuts to avoid bankruptcy.

5. The threatening weather is _____ our outdoor plans.

6. The encounter group _____ a definite change in attitudes among the participants.

7. Bringing computers into the classroom has _____ better writing.

8. The teachers' in service _____ an improved social studies curriculum.

9. Details of the candidate's private life _____ his ratings in the polls.

10. The student's excuse did not _____ the teacher's consequences.

11. The shoddy construction eventually _____ an accident which resulted in a lawsuit.

12. Hurricane Camille _____ the lives of thousands of people on the Gulf Coast.

As and Like

Like introduces a phrase and is a preposition. **As** and **as if** introduce clauses and are subordinating conjunctions. Although this distinction is often disregarded in informal speech, use *as* in formal, written language.

Examples: We need another dancer <u>like</u> him.
                        <u>As</u> I told you yesterday, you can't borrow the car.

Fill in the blanks with *like*, *as,* or *as if*.

1. **It looks _____ rain today.**

2. **It looks _____ it will rain today.**

3. **Damale, _____ her mother, is always late.**

4. **Your dog looks _____ a West Highland Terrier.**

5. **The student looked _____ he could fall asleep any minute.**

6. **She sounds _____ she is having an allergy attack.**

7. **_____ my brother, I have red hair.**

8. **Your backpack looks _____ mine.**

9. **Rebecca handles a tennis racket _____ a pro.**

10. **My vision is not as sharp _____ your vision is.**

11. **Mallory looked _____ she were ill.**

12. **He looked _____ he were going to cry.**

13. **She walked _____ she were in a trance.**

14. **The carousel looked _____ fun to the children.**

15. **The young child spoke _____ an adult.**

Between and Among

Between is used to describe the relationship of a person or thing to one other person or thing. Between can also refer to more than two persons or things when each person or object is considered in its relationship to others. **Among** is generally used when three or more persons or things are involved.

Examples: We divided the treats <u>between</u> Alex and Alyssa.
                 Cooperation <u>between</u> workers is essential in the workplace.
                 We divided the treats <u>among</u> the five children.

Read each sentence and write *between* or *among* as appropriate.

1. I see no difference in the quality _____ these two brands.

2. We need to choose soon from _____ all the applicants.

3. I'm sure that _____ the many choices at the pound, this dog is the perfect one for Nancy.

4. Let's keep that information _____ you and me.

5. There was a lot of tension _____ Marie and the other girls in the class.

6. We found the remote lodged _____ the two cushions.

7. It was hard to choose _____ the candidates because we didn't like any of them.

8. Walking through the forest, we saw a few sycamores _____ the elms.

9. _____ the many intriguing cookbooks on the bookstore shelf was a particularly intriguing one from Tuscany.

10. The treasures of the Uffizzi Museum in Florence are _____ the most beautiful pieces of art in the world.

11. The couple couldn't decide _____ Rome, Paris, or London for their honeymoon.

Lie and Lay

The verb **lie** means "to recline" and is intransitive (does not require a direct object). The verb **lay** means "put" and is transitive (requires a direct object) or must be in the passive voice. The principal parts of the verb are as follows:

basic form	past tense	past participle
lie	lay	lain
lay	laid	laid

Examples: She will <u>lie</u> in bed most of the morning. (basic form of lie in future tense)
After the long jog, I <u>lay</u> on the sofa for twenty minutes. (past tense of lie)
This memo has <u>lain</u> on the desk all day. (Past participle form of lie)
Please <u>lay</u> that crate on the floor. (basic form of lay in the present tense)
He <u>laid</u> the crate on the floor with a clatter. (past tense of lay)
He had <u>laid</u> the blame on me at that time. (past participle form of lay)
The book was <u>laid</u> on the shelf. (past form of lay in the passive voice)

Fill in the blank with the correct form of *lie* or *lay*.

1. The mountains _____ before us when we discovered car trouble.

2. The phone message has _____ unreturned for days.

3. I had _____ two dollars on the counter.

4. I like to _____ on my back in the sun for about twenty minutes.

5. Your bicycle has _____ on the sidewalk too long.

6. Chip _____ his books next to his locker.

7. How long has he _____ there?

8. I am going to _____ down.

9. _____ the keys where I can see them.

10. _____ down on the bed if you are tired.

11. I have _____ the papers somewhere and now I can't find them!

Word Usage

Sit and Set

Sit means "to place oneself" and is an intransitive verb that does not require an object.
Set means "to put" or "to place" and is a transitive verb, and requires an object or use in passive construction.

Example: Don't <u>sit</u> on the sofa in those sweaty clothes.
                    I <u>set</u> the remote on the coffee table.
                    The date was <u>set</u> last fall. (passive)

Exceptions: The sun <u>set</u>.
                    They <u>set</u> out at dawn.
                    Wait a few hours for the paint to <u>set</u>.

Fill in the blank with the correct form of *sit* or *set.*

1. _____ your purse on the counter and come here.

2. I will _____ my alarm for four in the morning.

3. I will _____ next to Kali at the movies.

4. We had been _____ at the gate for two hours before the flight was cancelled.

5. I will be _____ in the center balcony during the performance.

6. The crew _____ the stage as quickly as they could.

7. Don't _____ the clock until you check with the station.

8. I _____ my suitcase on the conveyor belt.

9. Mildred _____ the mail on my desk.

10. The company's sales _____ a record last week.

11. All we could do was _____ and wait.

12. Never _____ in Papa Bear's chair.

Commas

Comma usage does vary, but the following rules should be helpful:
1. Use a comma to separate independent clauses joined by the coordinating conjunctions *and, but, yet, neither, nor, or, so,* or *yet,* unless each clause is very short.

Examples: Brad will bring a variety of snacks, and Sarah will bring three or four videos.
The sky darkened, and the rain fell. (two short independent clauses)

2. Use a comma to separate a dependent (subordinate) clause from the main clause when the subordinate clause comes first. When the subordinate clause is in the middle, set it off with commas only if it is not essential to identifying the noun that precedes it.

Examples: The city in Louisiana which is the capital is Baton Rouge. (essential)
Baton Rouge, which is the capital of Louisiana, is in Cajun country.
(not essential)

Place commas where appropriate in each sentence. Some sentences need no commas.

1. **The chapter which comes next contains the scary part.**

2. **Chapter 24 which contains the scary part was assigned for homework.**

3. **Although they aren't millionaires they travel in style.**

4. **The room was tiny and the view was not so good.**

5. **The bed in the room was lumpy but she fell asleep anyway.**

6. **She must set the alarm or risk missing the train.**

7. **If she missed the train she would be late for a very important appointment.**

8. **Alex missed the ticketing deadline so his ticket was much more expensive.**

9. **When you read her resumé you'll see that she is well-qualified.**

10. **The man whom they met in Paris was from Afghanistan.**

Commas

Here are more uses for commas:
1. Use the **comma** to separate words, phrases, and clauses in a series.

Example: Stop, look, and listen.

2. Use a comma to separate two or more adjectives when they modify the same noun. *And, or*, or *nor* make commas unnecessary when they are placed between adjectives. If an adjective actually modifies the adjective that follows it as well as the noun, do not separate the adjectives with a comma.

Examples: Sherry was a loquacious, gregarious person. (modify same noun)
Sherry was loquacious and gregarious. (uses and between adjectives)
The garden was surrounded by an old stone fence. (1st adjective modifies 2nd adjective)

Add commas where they are appropriate. Some sentences do not need commas.

1. She has midterm exams this week in English Social Studies and Biology.

2. Do you need to change the size or style of the lettering?

3. The home is spacious and comfortable.

4. The speaker was nervous sweating and miserable.

5. The well-stocked grocery store contains anything you might need.

6. He was a cunning military analyst.

7. Trains in Germany are usually fast efficient comfortable and plentiful.

8. Pascali Pristine Fragrant Cloud and Brandy are some of my favorite roses.

9. Nathan dated Natalie Nicole Natasha Nancy Nina and Nadine in the same year.

10. Pecans chocolate chips butter sugar eggs and flour are in these cookies.

11. Eat drink and be merry!

12. Her campaign for governor was aggressive hard-hitting and expensive.

Colons

1. A colon can signal a reader's expectations about the text that follows:
   Example: Only one choice remained: do it myself.
2. A colon is used to introduce lists of words, phrases, and even clauses:
   Examples: There are three ingredients left to include: basil, cream, and salt.
   Candice's home is large: four bedrooms, three baths, a gameroom, computer room, and workout room.
   These steps are important before traveling abroad: get a passport, check to see if a visa is required, and exchange some currency in advance.
3. The colon is not used to introduce lists if the list is the object of the preposition, or object of the verb.
   Example: Sam went shopping for jeans, sweaters, and socks.

Add a colon in the appropriate place in each sentence. Do nothing if no colon is needed.

1. **A good vinaigrette needs these ingredients extra virgin olive oil, wine vinegar, Dijon mustard, and garlic.**

2. **John attributed his undeserved perfect score on the quiz to one thing luck.**

3. **Allen got a sprained ankle, sunburn, splinters, and an allergy attack during the hike.**

4. **Caution The undertow is strong.**

5. **The following teachers will be attending a conference today Ms. Pendleton, Mr. Rosinia, and Mrs. West.**

6. **Notice Drafts will count as 20% of your total score.**

7. **I am changing planes in Dallas, Salt Lake City, and Portland.**

8. **Two tasks remained before Janice could go to the movie complete her homework, and wash the dog.**

9. **His upcoming blind date was intriguing a former homecoming queen, class valedictorian, and a Karate blackbelt.**

10. **James will be applying to Princeton, University of Virginia, and Harvard.**

Colons

The following special situations use colons:
   1. Business letter salutations   *Dear Mr. Allen*:
   2. Title and subtitle   *Reading in the 90's: Improving Comprehension*
   3. Hours and minutes   *12:02 P.M.*
   4. Acts and scenes of play   *Hamlet, II:1*
   5. Publisher's location and name   *New York: McGraw-Hill*

Rewrite each of the following using a colon.

1. **six o'clock**

   _____

2. **Shakespeare (title) The Complete Works (subtitle)**

   _____

3. **The American Publishing Company in Hartford**

   _____

4. **page 6 in volume 2 of The History of the New World**

   _____

5. **Louisiana (title) The Land and Its People (subtitle)**

   _____

6. **Scene 2 in Act I of She Stoops to Conquer**

   _____

7. **Dear Sir**

   _____

8. **Rand McNally and Co. in Chicago**

   _____

9. **scene 3 in Act III of Our Town**

   _____

10. **ten o'clock**

   _____

Name _____ **Punctuation**

Quotation Marks

Quotation marks enclose the words used by a speaker or writer. Periods and commas go inside the closing quotation mark in the preferred American style, (although you may also see the British style which can vary). Question marks and exclamation points go inside the closing quotation marks when they apply only to the quoted words. Indirect quotations do not use quotation marks.

Examples:
"Come here," said Marie. (inside comma)
Marie said, "Come here." (inside period)
"Won't you come?" asked Marie. (question mark inside)
Did you hear Marie ask, "Won't you come"? (question mark outside)
Marie asked that I come. (indirect quotation)

Rewrite each sentence with quotation marks and appropriate placement of end punctuation.

1. **Look out yelled Pete.**

_____

2. **Stop saying Look out!**

_____

3. **The cashier said You need to have correct change.**

_____

4. **Do you know what time registration begins asked Laura.**

_____

5. **Did I actually hear her ask Who wants to skip class?**

_____

6. **Let's eat anchovy pizza tonight suggested Melanie.**

_____

7. **Alvin countered Let's either have Mexican food or a vegetarian meal.**

_____

© Carson Dellosa CD-3745   98

Answer Key

Name _____ Nouns

Concrete and Abstract

A **concrete noun** names an object which can be perceived by the senses.
An **abstract noun** names a quality, characteristic, or an idea.

Examples: Concrete: dress, fire, table, noise
           Abstract: democracy, hatred, beauty, happiness

Underline the concrete nouns and circle the abstract nouns in each sentence.

1. His (depression) continued long after the death of his wife.

2. The beggar felt (hunger) on a daily (basis).

3. The people witnessed the collision on their (way) to church.

4. The computer was left on by my sister.

5. (Yesterday) was rainy and overcast.

6. Will you graduate before the (end) of this (century)?

7. The magazine rack was overstuffed.

8. The dictionary on the desk is unabridged.

9. The crystal goblet fell and shattered.

10. The door was locked, and I had forgotten the key.

11. The people did not choose the harsh (dictatorship).

12. The paper was covered with finger paint.

13. The woman brought the ticket to her employer.

14. There is an anti-war (theme) to the novel.

13. The (strength) of the storm was impressive.

© Carson Dellosa CD-3745   1

Name _____ Nouns

Collective Nouns

A **collective noun** names a group as if it were one individual. The collective noun uses a singular verb when the group is referred to as a unit. It uses a plural verb when the individuals in the group are regarded separately.

Examples: The vote of the <u>committee</u> was unanimous. (singular)
                 The <u>committee</u> have continued to argue among themselves. (plural)

Underline the collective noun. In the blank write S if it is used as a singular noun or P if it is plural.

_S_ 1. The jury could not agree on a verdict in the case.

_P_ 2. The jury has its own reserved parking spaces.

_S_ 3. The new family next door has a West Highland White Terrier.

_P_ 4. The family were seated around the television.

_S_ 5. The crew has taken a vote and decided on a mutiny.

_P_ 6. The crew are coming on board to prepare their stations for the cruise.

_S_ 7. The majority has elected an independent candidate for president.

_P_ 8. The majority of the seniors are interested in a cruise for their class trip.

_S_ 9. The Jefferson High team won the division.

_P_ 10. After graduation, the team are going their separate ways.

Write a sentence using the collective noun "class" in the singular form. Write a second sentence using "class" as a plural collective noun.

1. Our class has a pet hamster.

2. All of the class were seated quietly.

© Carson Dellosa CD-3745   2

Name _____ Nouns

Plural Compound Nouns

Compound nouns form their plurals by adding s to the most important word in the compound noun.

Examples: mother-in-law   mothers-in-law
             wineglass   wineglasses

Write the plural form of each compound noun. Use a dictionary to check the spelling.

1. pogo stick _____ pogo sticks _____

2. baseball _____ baseballs _____

3. maitre d'hotel _____ maitres d'hotel _____

4. coup d'etat _____ coups d'etat _____

5. go-between _____ go-betweens _____

6. standby _____ standbys _____

7. printout _____ printouts _____

8. hanger-on _____ hangers-on _____

Write sentences using the compound nouns *bill of sale* and *manservant* in both their singular and plural forms.

1. Please write a bill of sale for me.

2. There are three bills of sale on the table.

3. Where is my manservant?

4. How many manservants do you have?

© Carson Dellosa CD-3745   3

Name _____ Nouns

Plural Compound Nouns

Compound nouns form their plurals by adding s to the most important word in the compound noun.

Examples: mother-in-law   mothers-in-law
             wineglass   wineglasses

Write the plural form of each compound noun. Use a dictionary to check the spelling.

1. father-in-law _____ fathers-in-law _____

2. will-o'-the-wisp _____ will-o'-the-wisps _____

3. toothbrush _____ toothbrushes _____

4. paintbrush _____ paintbrushes _____

5. hand-me-down _____ hand-me-downs _____

6. good-by _____ good-bys _____

7. stepmother _____ stepmothers _____

8. backpack _____ backpacks _____

Write sentences using the compound nouns *mother-in-law* and *hand-me-down* in both their singular and plural forms.

1. This is my mother-in-law.

2. They are all mothers-in law.

3. All I have to wear is a bunch of hand-me-downs.

4. This shirt is a hand-me-down from my brother.

© Carson Dellosa CD-3745   4

Answer Key

Plural Compound Nouns

Compound nouns form their plurals by adding s to the most important word in the compound noun.

Examples: mother-in-law   mothers-in-law
            wineglass   wineglasses

Write the plural form of each compound noun. Use a dictionary to check the spelling.

1. passerby _____ passersby _____
2. time-out _____ time-outs _____
3. toothbrush _____ toothbrushes _____
4. foothold _____ footholds _____
5. talisman _____ talismans _____
6. get-together _____ get-togethers _____
7. two-by-four _____ two-by-fours _____
8. handcuff _____ handcuffs _____

Write sentences using the compound nouns *passerby* and *toothbrush* in both their singular and plural forms.

1. He was only a passerby.
2. How many passersby did you see?
3. Don't forget your toothbrush.
4. Marge has two toothbrushes.

Plural Foreign Nouns

Some nouns of foreign origin that are commonly used in English retain the plural form of the language from which they came. Some use the typical English plurals -s and -es. Others have English and foreign forms.

Examples: Singular   English   Foreign
            vertebra   vertebras   vertebrae
            alumnus   alumni

Use a dictionary to determine the plural (or plurals) of each of the following nouns of foreign origin.

Singular	English Plural	Foreign Plural
1. stimulus		stimuli
2. synthesis		syntheses
3. synopsis		synopses
4. emphasis		emphases
5. diagnosis		diagnoses
6. radius	radiuses	radii
7. datum	datums	data
8. crisis		crises
9. syllabus	syllabuses	syllabi
10. genus		genera
11. agendum	agendums	agenda
12. parenthesis		parentheses

Plural Foreign Nouns

Some nouns of foreign origin that are commonly used in English retain the plural form of the language from which they came. Some use the typical English plurals -s and -es. Others have English and foreign forms.

Examples: Singular   English   Foreign
            datum   data
            tableau   tableaus   tableaux

Use a dictionary to determine the plural (or plurals) of each of the following nouns of foreign origin.

Singular	English Plural	Foreign Plural
1. matrix	matrixes	matrices
2. paparazzo		paparazzi
3. plateau	plateaus	plateaux
4. cranium	craniums	crania
5. momentum	momentums	momenta
6. nucleus	nucleuses	nuclei
7. prospectus		prospectuses
8. antenna	antennas	antennae
9. formula	formulas	formulae
10. basis		bases
11. curriculum	curriculums	curricula
12. axis		axes

Possessive Nouns

To make a singular noun **possessive**, add -s. If the noun ends in -s and is plural in meaning, add only an apostrophe. If the noun is singular in meaning, but ends in -s, add -'s.

Examples: Noun not ending in -s   the boy   the boy's basketball
          Noun ending in -s   the boss   the boss's temper
          Plural noun   the bosses   the bosses' meeting
          Irregular Plurals   children   children's toys

An exception is made in the case of words in which an extra s would make pronunciation difficult such as "for goodness' sake." In that case, add only an apostrophe.

The singular form of each noun below is given. Write the other forms requested.

singular	singular possessive	plural	plural possessive
1. book	book's	books	books'
2. hem	hem's	hems	hems'
3. exercise	exercise's	exercises	exercises'
4. company	company's	companies	companies'
5. piano	piano's	pianos	pianos'
6. movie	movie's	movies	movies'
7. waitress	waitress's	waitresses	waitresses'
8. lady	lady's	ladies	ladies'
9. dormouse	dormouse's	dormice	dormice's
10. life	life's	lives	lives'

Answer Key

Name _____ **Nouns**

Possessive Nouns

To make a singular noun **possessive**, add -s. If the noun ends in -s and is plural in meaning, add only an apostrophe. If the noun is singular in meaning, but ends in -s, add -'s.

Examples:
Noun not ending in -s   the boy   the boy's basketball
Noun ending in -s   the boss   the boss's temper
Plural noun   the bosses   the bosses' meeting
Irregular Plurals   children   children's toys

An exception is made in the case of words in which an extra s would make pronunciation difficult such as "for goodness' sake." In that case, add only an apostrophe.

The singular form of each noun below is given. Write the other forms requested.

singular	singular possessive	plural	plural possessive
1. book	book's	books	books'
2. costume	costume's	costumes	costumes'
3. church	church's	churches	churches'
4. cloak	cloak's	cloaks	cloaks'
5. test	test's	tests	tests'
6. hurricane	hurricane's	hurricanes	hurricanes'
7. briefcase	briefcase's	briefcases	briefcases'
8. goose	goose's	geese	geese's
9. cliff	cliff's	cliffs	cliffs'
10. fedora	fedora's	fedoras	fedoras'

9

Name _____ **Pronouns**

Types of Pronouns

Pronouns take the place of nouns. There are several kinds.
1. **Personal pronouns** include forms of 1st, 2nd, and 3rd person: *I, mine, me, we, ours, us, you, yours, he, she, it, his, hers, its, him, her, they, theirs,* and *them.*
2. **Indefinite pronouns** refer to persons or things generally: *anybody, few, most, neither, no one, nothing, several, etc.*
3. **Demonstrative pronouns** refer to persons or things specifically: *this, that, these,* and *those.*
4. **Relative pronouns** connect a dependent clause to the main clause and function as the subject or object of the dependent clause: *who, which, that, whose, whom.* The ending -*ever* can be added to each form.
5. **Reflexive pronouns** are formed by adding -*self* or -*selves* to the personal pronouns (except for *himself, ourself, theirself,* and *theirselves.*) Pronouns are reflexive when the same person or thing is both the subject and object. (Intensive pronouns use the same forms, but simply emphasize a noun or pronoun without adding new meaning.)
6. **Reciprocal pronouns** express shared feelings or actions: *each other, one another.*

Read each sentence and identify the underlined word as: personal (P), indefinite (I), demonstrative (D), relative (REL), reflexive (REF), or reciprocal (REC).

__P__ 1. They enjoyed the movie very much.

__P__ 2. What did she say?

__P__ 3. Rachel thought the purse was mine.

__D__ 4. This is a group of volunteers who are indispensable.

__REF__ 5. Maria saw herself on the evening news.

__REC__ 6. The brothers helped each other.

__I__ 7. Has anyone offered to help?

__I__ 8. Joy knows everyone at school.

__P__ 9. Who will go with me tonight?

10

Name _____ **Pronouns**

Changing Nouns to Pronouns

In each sentence choose a pronoun to take the place of the underlined words and write it on the line. Choose from the following types of pronouns: personal (PER), possessive (POS), demonstrative (DEM), indefinite (IND), and reflexive (REF).

__these__ 1. Ms. Rausch asked what scene had a need for the rifles.
(DEM)

__Their__ 2. The entrance of the soldiers in Act I was very effective.
(PER)

__themselves__ 3. The soldiers were pleased with their performance.
(REF)

__she__ 4. Then Carmen made her appearance.
(PER)

__it__ 5. The stage director kept running through Act I over and over.
(PER)

__this__ 6. The singers muttered objections to the repeated run throughs.
(DEM)

__theirs__ 7. The urchins were not comfortable with their music yet, but the school girls in Act IV were comfortable with the part.
(POS)

__Everyone__ 8. The members of the chorus sounded terrific.
(IND)

__them__ 9. An entrance down the stairs was made by the cigarette girls.
(PER)

__They__ 10. The choral and stage directors were working twelve hour days.
(PER)

__themselves__ 11. The principals were pleased with their performance.
(REF)

__them__ 12. The audience gave the performers a standing ovation.
(PER)

11

Name _____ **Verbs**

Auxiliary Verbs

Auxiliary verbs, also called helping verbs, always accompany a main verb. An auxiliary verb helps the main verb to express tense, voice, or mood, but usually has little meaning of its own. Some examples include *be, do, have, can, might, would, may, will* and *must.* If an auxiliary verb is used alone, it is not an auxiliary verb in that sentence. A combination of two or more verbs is called a verb phrase. Verb phrases contain at least one auxiliary verb. Adverbs may appear in the middle of a verb phrase, but are not part of it.

Examples:
We are waiting in a long line.
I did go with him.
I would have gone.
I have been walking.
I could hardly wait.

Underline the main verb once. Underline the auxiliary verb(s) twice.

1. Elmer has rarely exhibited a bad temper.

2. The county will try the case next month.

3. The man had received no driver's license.

4. I could not complete the task in that length of time.

5. Those girls are known as the Baxter twins.

6. The cat was playing with the drapery cord.

7. The popularity of that product has risen for months.

8. The Empire State Building was used as a set in many famous movies.

9. The Twin Towers is now dominating the New York skyline.

10. We will begin the long drive early in the morning.

11. I have been jogging with Alex for two years.

12. Do you know the coach?

12

Answer Key

Page 13

Name _____ Verbs

Linking Verbs

Linking verbs describe conditions instead of actions. They are followed by words that rename or describe the subject. Forms of the verb *to be* are most commonly used as linking verbs. Some other verbs used as linking verbs are *appear, become, feel, grow, look, prove, remain, seem,* and *turn.* These verbs do not function as linking verbs if they do not describe conditions that are followed by a word that renames or describes the subject.

Examples: Carla <u>is</u> my only sister. (linking)
Carla's friend <u>is</u> running for governor. (auxiliary)
Bob <u>grew</u> sleepy during the long lecture. (linking)
Roger <u>grew</u> beautiful roses in his garden. (action)

Read each sentence. If the verb is linking, write L in the blank. If the verb is not linking, write NL.

L 1. The roar of the sea <u>was</u> imposing.

NL 2. The roar of the sea <u>was</u> <u>heard</u> far away.

L 3. Mandy <u>looks</u> pretty in pink.

NL 4. Mandy <u>looked</u> behind the sofa for the remote.

NL 5. Valerie <u>appeared</u> on a local television show last night.

L 6. Valerie <u>appeared</u> anxious about her exam.

L 7. Jennifer <u>felt</u> uncomfortable with the new crowd.

NL 8. Jennifer <u>felt</u> the child's feverish forehead.

L 9. The wasp nest <u>is</u> near the door.

L 10. The wasp nest <u>is</u> a scary sight to the child.

NL 11. Evacuation plans <u>were</u> <u>devised</u> in advance of the hurricane.

L 12. The evacuation plans <u>were</u> unclear.

© Carson Dellosa CD-3745   13

Page 14

Name _____ Verbs

Irregular Verbs

The principle parts of a verb are the three forms upon which all tenses are based.

<u>Present</u> <u>Past</u> <u>Past Participle</u> (auxiliary verb needed)
love loved loved

Many frequently used verbs have principle parts that are irregularly formed.

<u>Present</u> <u>Past</u> <u>Past Participle</u> (auxiliary verb needed)
drive drove driven

Look at the present form of the verb given. Fill in the other two forms. Use a dictionary to check your work.

Present	Past	Past Participle
1. lay	laid	laid
2. speak	spoke	spoken
3. forsake	forsook	forsaken
4. lie	lay	lain
5. begin	began	begun
6. rise	rose	risen
7. swear	swore	sworn
8. fly	flew	flown
9. slay	slayed	slain
10. grind	ground	ground
11. shake	shook	shaken
12. string	strung	strung

© Carson Dellosa CD-3745   14

Page 15

Name _____ Verbs

Irregular Verbs

The principle parts of a verb include present (infinitive), past and past participle. Regular verbs form the past tense by adding *-ed,* and the past participle form by adding *-ed* plus at least one auxiliary verb. **Irregular verbs** form the past and past participle in ways other than *-ed,* although the past participle must still be used with one or more auxiliary verbs.

Example: <u>Infinitive</u> <u>Past</u> <u>Past Participle</u>
to drive drove driven

Write the irregular verb form that is requested in each of the following sentences. P indicates that past is requested, and PP indicates that the past participle is requested.

1. draw (PP)—Elizabeth had _____drawn_____ a geometric design on her notebook.

2. forgive (P)—Jo _____forgave_____ Amy for burning her manuscript.

3. do (PP)—Russell had _____done_____ his homework before he went to the movie.

4. write (P)—William Golding _____wrote_____ *Lord of the Flies.*

5. tear (PP)—The toddler has _____torn_____ her favorite book.

6. wind (P)—The path _____wound_____ around the lake.

7. swear (P)—The witness _____swore_____ that he would tell the truth.

8. set (PP)—I had _____set_____ the clock properly, but the electricity went out.

9. ring (PP)—The bell had _____rung_____ before Stacey got off the bus.

10. ride (P)—Lauren _____rode_____ the gentle mare on the beach.

© Carson Dellosa CD-3745   15

Page 16

Name _____ Verbs

Simple Verb Tense

The **tense** of the verb shows the time of an action. The simple **present tense** shows that an action takes place now at the same time that it is being described. It is also used to describe habitual action, to tell general truths, or to write about books, movies and other narratives. It can also be used to indicate a time in the future. The **past tense** shows that an action took place at some previous time. The **future tense** shows the action will take place at some time to come.

Examples: The child <u>fills</u> her dog's bowl daily with fresh water. (present)
The people <u>elect</u> their government in a democratic society. (present)
I <u>leave</u> for Costa Rica tomorrow. (present)
He <u>filled</u> the glasses and everyone toasted. (past)
Jenny <u>will fill</u> the garden with bright flowers. (future)

Underline the complete verb. Determine the tense (present, past, or future) and write it on the line provided.

present 1. The family frequents the beach all summer.

present 2. I see a wide variety of flora and fauna at the wildlife preserve.

present 3. In the musical *The Secret Garden,* Mary Lennox sings with Archibald Dickon and the ghost of Lilly.

past 4. The city finally started a recycling program.

future 5. These opera glasses will really help you see the performance.

past 6. Drew misplaced the portable phone again.

past 7. We danced until the clock struck midnight.

future 8. The dog will not bite someone as nice as you.

future 9. The network will broadcast the game live on Saturday night.

present 10. The washing machine repairman is finally here.

© Carson Dellosa CD-3745   16

Answer Key

Name _____   **Verbs**

Present Perfect Tense

The **present perfect tense** shows that an action began in the past and extends to the present or is completed in the present.

Examples: I <u>am filling</u> all the glasses. (simple present)
              I <u>have filled</u> all the water glasses. (present perfect)

              Jane runs three miles every day. (simple present)
              Jane has run three miles every day for two weeks. (present perfect)

Read each sentence and determine its tense. Write SP in the blank for simple present or PP for present perfect.

_SP_   1. Harry washes the car on Thursdays.

_PP_   2. Maude has seen that movie many times.

_SP_   3. I go to the dentist twice a year.

_PP_   4. I have been going to the dentist twice a year for quite some time now.

_PP_   5. Jane has written an article for the school news paper.

_PP_   6. I have known her since she was a child.

_SP_   7. We have three kittens.

_PP_   8. I have had two colds this year so far.

_PP_   9. He has taken the last bite.

_SP_ 10. Today is my birthday.

_SP_ 11. The cat is in the tree.

_PP_ 12. She has studied for the test all weekend.

     17

Name _____   **Verbs**

Past Perfect Tense

The **past perfect tense** shows that an action was completed before another action in the past or completed before a definite time in the past. It is formed by using *had* and the past participle form of the verb.

Example: I <u>had run</u> five miles a day before the jogging accident.

Read each sentence. Underline the complete verb. If the tense of the verb is past perfect, write PP in the blank.

_____   1. Jeanette <u>has frequented</u> the mall since she was thirteen.

_____   2. Jeanette <u>frequented</u> the mall after school.

_PP_   3. Jeanette <u>had frequented</u> the mall until her mother took her credit cards.

_____   4. The old woman <u>walked</u> with difficulty.

_PP_   5. The old woman <u>had walked</u> with difficulty for years.

_____   6. The train <u>ran</u> late.

_PP_   7. The train <u>had run</u> late on that fateful night.

_____   8. That train <u>has run</u> late often.

_PP_   9. The graffiti <u>had been</u> unsightly on the subway walls until the walls were freshly painted.

_____ 10. The graffiti <u>has covered</u> the subway walls of Paris for years.

Rewrite the following sentences in the past perfect tense.

1. I have known the waiter at Brennan's for years.

    I had known the waiter at Brennan's for years.

2. Ralph attended Clearwater High School.

    Ralph had attended Clearwater High School.

     18

Name _____   **Verbs**

Future Perfect Tense

The **future perfect tense** shows that an action will be completed in the future before another action in the future or before a given time in the future. The future perfect combines the auxiliary verbs *will* and *have* with the past participle of the main verb.

Example: The jury will convict the defendant. (simple future)
              They <u>will have convicted</u> the defendant by now. (future perfect)

Put a check in the blank before each sentence that is in the future perfect tense.

✓   1. By next year Roger and Patricia will have built their own log cabin.

_____   2. They will continue to try to stop you from making mistakes.

✓   3. In a few years the Octogenarian Club will have been decimated.

_____   4. Roger and Patricia will build a log cabin as a summer home.

_____   5. The squirrels will collect a supply of nuts throughout the orchard.

✓   6. Andrew will have returned home by 11 o'clock.

Write each of the following sentences in the future perfect tense. Be sure to connect each to another event in the future or a specified time.

1. The baby will eat solid food.

    By Christmas, the baby will have eaten solid food.

2. The group of girls will walk to the mall.

    The group of girl will have walked to the mall by two o'clock.

     19

Name _____   **Verbs**

Progressive Form

All verb tenses have a progressive form. The **progressive form** combines an auxiliary verb with the present participle form of the verb which ends in *-ing*. This form emphasizes continuing action or action in progress.

Examples: I <u>am running</u> more often now. (present progressive)
           He <u>was running</u> when he saw Alice. (past progressive)
           I <u>will be running</u> every Tuesday. (future progressive)
           I <u>have been running</u> all summer. (present perfect progress.)
           He <u>had been running</u> for years until his injury. (past perfect progressive)
           She <u>will have been taking</u> ballet lessons for 10 years before becoming a teaching assistant. (future perfect progressive)

Identify each of the following sentences by the letter of the correct progressive form. If the form is not progressive, write NP.

A) present progressive   D) present perfect progressive
B) past progressive   E) past perfect progressive
C) future progressive   F) future perfect progressive

_B_   1. Janet <u>was looking</u> in the phone directory for an auto repair shop.

_C_   2. The librarian <u>will be waiting</u> for you to finish the make-up exam.

_A_   3. I <u>am taking</u> advanced English this year.

_E_   4. Greg <u>had been looking</u> forward to the prom, until his date got the flu.

_D_   5. The manager <u>has been working</u> with the employees to boost sales.

_F_   6. By June, Elaine <u>will have been volunteering</u> at the hospital for fifteen years.

_B_   7. Babies <u>were crawling</u> all over the room at the day care center.

_A_   8. I <u>am going</u> to your house today.

_NP_   9. Meghan <u>has found</u> the right canopy for her bed.

_D_ 10. The child <u>has been refusing</u> to eat green peas for years.

     20

Answer Key

Name _____ Verbs

Verb Tense Review

Read the sentences and underline the complete verb for each. Select the letter of the correct verb tense and write it on the line before each sentence.

A.	Simple Present	G.	Present Progressive
B.	Simple Past	H.	Past Progressive
C.	Simple Future	I.	Future Progressive
D.	Present Perfect	J.	Present Perfect Progressive
E.	Past Perfect	K.	Past Perfect Progressive
F.	Future Perfect	L.	Future Perfect Progressive

H 1. She was watering the garden too much.

L 2. Nick will have been teaching for fifteen years by the time he retires..

E 3. The leading lady had not missed one rehearsal since January.

B 4. I will have graduated by the year 2025.

G 5. Jody is dragging his dog away from the cat.

I 6. Students will be using calculators for complex math problems.

J 7. I have been doing my best with this project.

C 8. I will think about that comment.

A 9. Give me a break.

K 10. We had been playing soccer when she fell and broke her leg.

D 11. The weather has been a factor in our plans.

E 12. Had you studied hard for that test?

H 13. The students were studying for the test during lunch.

B 14. Jack located the most foreign phrases for the assignment.

© Carson-Dellosa CD-3745   21

Name _____ Verbs

Verb Tense Review

Rewrite the following sentences in the tense requested.

1. Rafael will be arriving by plane at 6 o'clock.
(change to present progressive)
   Rafael is arriving by plane at 6 o'clock.

2. Mark had avoided his friend all afternoon.
(change to present progressive)
   Mark is avoiding his friend all afternoon.

3. Manuel tended the garden with loving care.
(change to simple future)
   Manuel will tend the garden with loving care.

4. Adam was snoring loudly on the couch all afternoon.
(change to present perfect)
   Adam has snored loudly on the couch all afternoon.

5. Margot and Jack will have been dating for two years on Valentine's Day.
(change to past perfect progressive)
   Margot and Jack had been dating for two years on Valentine's Day.

6. The thief has been caught with the cookie in her hand.
(change to simple past)
   The thief was caught with the cookie in her hand.

7. I will be happy to go with you.
(change to simple present)
   I am happy to go with you.

© Carson-Dellosa CD-3745   22

Name _____ Verbs

Verb Tense Review

Write a sentence with the verb given in the tense indicated.

1. (to run—past perfect) Ann had run beside me for eight miles.

2. (to see—simple present) I see something in the window.

3. (to go—future progressive) She will be going alone.

4. (to drive—past progressive) We were driving to Grandma's house.

5. (to help—simple past) Nathan helped me write my paper.

6. (to smile—future perfect) I will have smiled for that picture two times now.

7. (to fall—simple future) He will fall if he gets too high.

8. (to work—present perfect) We have worked a total of five hours.

9. (to swim—future progressive) Will you be swimming on the team?

© Carson-Dellosa CD-3745   23

Name _____ Verbs

Transitive and Intransitive Verbs

The classification of verbs is directly related to how they function with subjects and objects. **Transitive verbs** require a direct object to complete their meanings. If the question "Who?" or "What?" can be answered after an action verb, the verb is transitive. **Intransitive verbs** express an action that is complete in itself and are often followed by a prepositional phrase. Some verbs can be used as either transitive or intransitive. Linking verbs are never transitive.

Examples: The race began. (Intransitive)
    Meghan began *The Giver* last week. (Transitive)
    The feature began at 3 o'clock. (Intransitive)
    She is the winner. (Intransitive)

For each sentence below, circle the transitive verbs and underline the intransitive verbs.

1. Betty (ate) the whole pie.

2. The teacher (wanted) the answer too quickly.

3. Chloe is a citizen of the United States.

4. Salvador (described) the diamond brooch in great detail.

5. The cat always slept under the bed.

6. The content of the editorial was unsettling.

7. The Belgian man (married) an Egyptian women.

8. The evidence is compelling in this case.

9. The Morrison family lives in the suburbs.

10. Allison (understood) the concept very well.

11. Mark ran into a problem at work today.

12. Mark (ran) five miles every morning.

© Carson-Dellosa CD-3745   24

Answer Key

Name _____ **Verbs**

Active and Passive Verbs

A verb is **active** when the subject is the doer of the action. A verb is **passive** when the subject is the receiver of the action.

Example: The fireman <u>rescued</u> the baby from the burning building. (active)
The baby <u>was rescued</u> from the burning building. (passive)

Identify each sentence as active (A) or passive (P). If it is active, rewrite it as passive. If it is passive, rewrite it as active.

__P__ 1. The prescription was filled by the pharmacist.

    <u>The pharmacist filled the prescription.</u>

__A__ 2. The children pitied the stray dog.

    <u>The stray dog was pitied by the children.</u>

__P__ 3. The proceeds from the fundraiser were deposited by the treasurer.

    <u>The treasurer deposited the proceeds from the fundraiser.</u>

__A__ 4. Cedrick left a message on my voice mail.

    <u>A message from Cedrick was left on my voice mail.</u>

__A__ 5. The movie critic reviewed the new release.

    <u>The new release was reviewed by the movie critic.</u>

__A__ 6. My brother ordered salad as an appetizer.

    <u>Salad was ordered by my brother as an appetizer.</u>

__A__ 7. The audience applauded the tenor's solo.

    <u>The tenor's solo was applauded by the audience.</u>

25

Name _____ **Verbs**

Active and Passive Verbs

A verb is **active** when the subject is the doer of the action. A verb is **passive** when the subject is the receiver of the action.

Examples: The fireman <u>rescued</u> the baby from the burning building. (active)
The baby <u>was rescued</u> from the burning building. (passive)

Identify each sentence as active (A) or passive (P).

__A__ 1. Perry believed the tall tale.

__A__ 2. The small craft sank in the storm.

__A__ 3. Clothilde waited for the signal.

__P__ 4. The banana split was devoured by the young child.

__P__ 5. The short story was written by an eighth grader.

__A__ 6. The wind damaged the roof of the garage.

__A__ 7. The honest person returned my wallet.

__P__ 8. My wallet was returned by the honest person.

__A__ 9. The son was running the business now.

__P__ 10. The business was run by the youngest son.

__P__ 11. The rumor was denied by her classmates.

__A__ 12. Her classmates denied the rumor.

__P__ 13. The purse was found in the cloakroom.

__A__ 14. The janitor found the missing purse.

__A__ 15. The Red Cross aided the flood victims.

26

Name _____ **Adjectives**

Descriptive, Limiting, and Pronominal Adjectives

An **adjective** modifies a noun (or pronoun). There are several kinds. **Descriptive adjectives** describe or characterize a noun by making the meaning more precise. There are also two kinds of limiting **adjectives** called definite and indefinite articles. The indefinite article the specifies a particular noun. The indefinite articles a and an generalize the noun. Adjectives derived from pronoun forms are called **pronominal adjectives.**

Examples: <u>shabby</u> couch (descriptive) <u>the</u> truth (limiting)
<u>Catholic</u> priest (descriptive) <u>a</u> sign (limiting)
<u>this</u> time (pronominal) <u>an</u> apple (limiting)
<u>which</u> direction (pronominal) <u>some</u> days (pronominal)
<u>its</u> cover (pronominal)

Underline each adjective and classify it as D for descriptive, L for limiting, or P for pronominal. The first one has been done for you.

1. The <u>African</u> safari took us through <u>a</u> <u>magnificent</u> <u>wildlife</u> preserve.

2. Amy wore <u>a</u> <u>white</u> blouse with <u>a</u> <u>straight</u> skirt and <u>wide</u> belt.

3. <u>Whose</u> picture is in <u>the</u> <u>newspaper</u>?

4. <u>The</u> choice of colors was <u>a</u> <u>big</u> mistake.

5. <u>Every</u> girl in <u>the</u> room was over thirteen.

6. <u>The</u> <u>May</u> flood will not soon be forgotten by <u>New Orleans</u> residents.

7. <u>Some</u> people had <u>eighteen</u> inches of water in <u>their</u> houses.

8. I can't decide <u>which</u> <u>luscious</u> dessert to choose.

9. <u>The</u> <u>flamenco</u> dancer was appearing nightly in Granada.

10. I can't decide <u>which</u> computer to choose for <u>home</u> use.

11. <u>Her</u> father muttered about <u>the</u> <u>outrageous</u> prices of <u>school</u> textbooks.

12. <u>The</u> cab <u>which</u> we liked best was driven by <u>an</u> <u>older</u> man.

27

Name _____ **Adjectives**

Predicate Adjectives

Adjectives that describe the subject, but follow the linking verb are called **predicate adjectives.**

Example: The designer purse is expensive. (predicate adjective)

Designer and expensive both describe the purse. Note that designer is a descriptive adjective, because it precedes the noun it describes, and expensive is a predicate adjective because it comes after the subject and it follows a linking verb.

Read each sentence. Underline each descriptive adjective and circle each predicate adjective.

1. Her <u>cherished</u> scrapbook was filled with <u>special</u> mementos.

2. Malcolm's actions were (inexcusable).

3. The <u>weary</u> soldier looked (excited) at the thought of rest.

4. The <u>chocolate</u> cake was (scrumptious).

5. Sharon bought her <u>school</u> supplies at the <u>last</u> minute.

6. The <u>classroom</u> dictionary was (worn).

7. The <u>rambunctious</u> cat tangled the <u>curtain</u> cords.

8. The <u>wildlife</u> calendar was (stunning).

9. Jack is a <u>successful</u> architect.

10. The <u>crystal</u> vase shattered on the <u>marble</u> floor.

11. The teacher became (annoyed) with the <u>noise</u> level.

12. The kindergartner looked (angelic) but was not.

28

Answer Key

Name _____   **Adjectives**

Pronominal Adjectives

Pronominal adjectives are pronouns that are used as adjectives. Demonstrative forms (*this, that, these,* and *those*) refer to objects that have already been mentioned or can be pointed out. Interrogative forms such as *what, which* and *whose* modify a noun in the context of a question. Relative forms such as *whose* or *which* introduce a subordinate clause and modify a noun in the clause. Indefinite forms such as *any, some, every, each, other, neither,* and *both* modify a noun in a nonspecific way. Possessive forms such as *my, your, his, her, their,* and *its* show possession of the noun that follows.

Examples: This booksack is worn. (demonstrative)
                What time did you arrive? (interrogative)
                Choose which color you like. (relative)
                Each selection looked intriguing. (indefinite)
                He felt the sting of her words. (possessive)

Look at the italicized pronominal adjective in each sentence and classify it as demonstrative (D), interrogative (INT), relative (REL), indefinite (IND), or possessive (PO).

PO 1. *Your* hair needs brushing.

INT 2. *Which* brother is the handsome one?

INT 3. *Whose* book is on the table?

IND 4. Do you have *any* fax paper?

PO 5. *Their* noses were really sunburned.

D 6. *These* Belgian chocolates are delectable.

INT 7. *Whose* picture is in your locker?

REL 8. Valerie didn't know *which* invitation arrived first.

IND 9. *Neither* day is good for me.

D 10. I couldn't find *those* scissors in my sewing box.

     29

Name _____   **Adjectives**

Comparison Adjectives

The three degrees of comparison of adjectives are **positive, comparative,** and **superlative.** The comparative degree shows the relationship between two persons, objects or ideas. The superlative degree shows the relationship among three or more.
The change is commonly indicated by the endings *-er* and *-est* in one syllable adjectives. *More* and *most* or *less* and *least* are used to form comparatives and superlatives when adjectives contain more than two syllables. Some adjectives that contain two syllables can form comparisons either way, but some can only use *more* and *most* or *less* and *least.*

Examples:

Positive	Comparative	Superlative
small	smaller	smallest
narrow	narrower	narrowest
handsome	more handsome	most handsome

Fill in the blank with the correct comparative form of the adjective.

1. (high) One of the towers was _____ higher _____ than the other.

2. (practical) His suggestion was the _____ most practical _____ of all the solutions.

3. (wise) The adage was _____ wiser _____ than his friends' advice.

4. (rapid) The noon train was _____ more rapid _____ than any of the others.

5. (thick) Melba chose the _____ thicker _____ novel of the two.

6. (cheap) This model of the appliance is the _____ cheapest _____.

7. (handsome) Harold is _____ more handsome _____ than his brother.

8. (adventurous) Mark is _____ more adventurous _____ than his brother Mike.

9. (distinct) The print on this copy is the _____ most distinct _____ of any of them.

10. (modest) This bathing suit is _____ more modest _____ than that one.

     30

Name _____   **Adjectives**

Irregular Comparisons

Some adjectives are not logically capable of comparison in formal speech and writing because their meaning is **absolute** (e.g., fatal, complete etc.), although some of these can be modified by adverbs such as *more, less, nearly,* or *virtually.* Example: Jasmine's design was even *more* unique.

Look at each adjective. If it can be generally compared by degree, write C. If it is usually an absolute, write A.

A 1. empty   **C** 9. exotic   **A** 17. infinite

C 2. kind   **A** 10. perfect   **C** 18. pious

A 3. final   **C** 11. sturdy   **C** 19. weird

C 4. remote   **C** 12. promising   **C** 20. fine

C 5. serene   **A** 13. round   **C** 21. skillful

A 6. complete   **A** 14. universal   **C** 22. efficient

C 7. lovely   **A** 15. correct   **A** 23. wrong

C 8. evil   **A** 16. eternal   **A** 24. single

Choose 5 absolutes and write a sentence with each one.

1. Last summer I saw the Eternal Flame.

2. Now my work is complete!

3. You have the correct answer.

4. This dress is perfect for my wedding.

5. The garbage can is empty.

     31

Name _____   **Adjectives**

Adjective Review

In each sentence, look at the underlined adjective. Write what type of adjective it is in the blank. Use the following abbreviations:

     (D) demonstrative   **(I) interrogative**   **(R) relative**
     (IND) indefinite   **(P) possessive**   **(DES) descriptive**

D 1. This book is so interesting.

D 2. That is the girl who won the math contest.

R 3. I don't know which pencil to use.

DES 4. I saw a really scary movie late last night.

P 5. My big sister helps me with my homework.

I 6. Whose sweater is this?

D 7. Is this play going to last much longer?

DES 8. He has a big head.

IND 9. Each person should bring his own lunch.

DES 10. I love this little white kitten.

D 11. I want this bike for my birthday.

P 12. Your hair is a mess.

P 13. Their way is the wrong way.

IND 14. Neither one is what I really want.

INT 15. Which night is good for you?

     32

Answer Key

Name _____ **Adverbs**

Adverbs

An **adverb** is a word used to modify a verb, adjective, or another adverb. Some adverbs are formed from adjectives and simply add *-ly*, but many do not. Adverbs answer a variety of questions about the word they modify including *How, How often, To what degree, When,* and *Where*. An adverb can be a single word, a phrase, or a clause.

Examples:
The volunteers worked <u>selflessly</u>. (how)
I return to my hometown <u>occasionally</u>. (how often)
She seemed <u>very</u> knowledgeable. (to what degree)
You can go <u>tomorrow</u>. (when)
He travels <u>everywhere</u>. (where)

A simple adverb is underlined in each sentence. Circle the word it modifies. Identify the word it modifies as a verb (V), adjective (ADJ), or another adverb (ADV).

<u>ADV</u> 1. Playing the guitar was <u>much</u> (too) difficult for the five year old.

<u>V</u> 2. That scheming opportunist (was) <u>once</u> my friend.

<u>ADJ</u> 3. Please give a <u>very</u> (generous) donation to the fundraiser for Children's Hospital.

<u>ADJ</u> 4. A unicycle has <u>only</u> (one) wheel.

<u>V</u> 5. The students from Washington Junior High (visit) the library <u>regularly</u>.

<u>V</u> 6. I (saw) him <u>once</u>, and it was unforgettable.

<u>V</u> 7. Vinnie <u>always</u> (jogs) in Central Park on the weekend.

<u>ADJ</u> 8. The national debt is becoming <u>increasingly</u> (important) to the electorate.

<u>V</u> 9. The hot dogs (burned) <u>quickly</u> on the barbecue pit.

<u>V</u> 10. The snow goose (flew) <u>east</u>.

33

Name _____ **Adverbs**

Intensifiers

Adverbs usually modify the verb by telling *where, when, how, to what degree,* and *under what conditions*. Adjectives modify or describe nouns and pronouns. Adverbs that modify other adverbs or adjectives are called **intensifiers**.

Examples:
Matt fell <u>very</u> awkwardly to the ground.
She is a <u>really</u> pretty girl.

Underline the intensifier. If it modifies an adverb, write ADV in the blank. If it modifies an adjective, write ADJ.

<u>ADJ</u> 1. Scarlet O'Hara's waist was <u>exceptionally</u> small.

<u>ADV</u> 2. The phone rang <u>most</u> frequently between five and six.

<u>ADV</u> 3. The message sounded <u>extremely</u> urgent.

<u>ADV</u> 4. Curry is a spice <u>quite</u> commonly found in Indian food.

<u>ADJ</u> 5. The <u>very</u> tired runner collapsed.

<u>ADJ</u> 6. Virginia had a <u>really</u> suspicious look on her face.

<u>ADV</u> 7. His mood changed <u>too</u> quickly.

<u>ADV</u> 8. The winner acted <u>rather</u> conceited.

<u>ADJ</u> 9. The storyteller always told <u>completely</u> unbelievable tales.

<u>ADJ</u> 10. The speech was <u>exceedingly</u> tedious.

<u>ADJ</u> 11. The beach was <u>extraordinarily</u> hot.

<u>ADV</u> 12. I can come <u>almost</u> any time.

<u>ADJ</u> 13. She is <u>somewhat</u> smarter in trigonometry than Ralph.

<u>ADJ</u> 14. The situation grew <u>increasingly</u> desperate.

<u>ADJ</u> 15. Jeff complained about the <u>absolutely</u> awful movie.

34

Name _____ **Prepositions**

Identifying Prepositions

Prepositions connect nouns and pronouns to other words in a sentence and show their relationship. Prepositions never stand alone. They introduce a prepositional phrase that contains a noun or pronoun and its modifiers.

Examples:
spoon <u>*under* the kitchen table</u>
morning <u>*before* the wedding</u>
bird <u>*in* the sycamore tree</u>

Fill in the blank with a preposition. Underline the phrase it introduces.

1. The memorable part was sung ____**by**____ <u>the amazing tenor</u>.

2. The inconspicuous woman ____**in**____ <u>the blue dress</u> shoplifted an expensive watch.

3. Baton Rouge is the capital ____**of**____ <u>Louisiana</u>.

4. The coffee ____**from**____ <u>Brazil</u> was the most aromatic.

5. The rest ____**of**____ <u>the ice cream</u> mysteriously disappeared.

6. The book was ____**about**____ <u>the War of the Roses</u>.

7. The shutters rattled loudly ____**during**____ <u>the storm</u>.

8. The whole class is going ____**with**____ <u>the teacher</u>.

9. The news spread ____**across**____ <u>the countryside</u>.

10. No one knew what was ____**behind**____ <u>those mountains</u>.

11. The remote was firmly lodged ____**between**____ <u>the cushions</u>.

12. I wondered what was happening ____**in**____ <u>the huddle</u>.

13. The unearthly noise ____**inside**____ <u>the house</u> unnerved everyone.

14. The telephone message ____**of**____ <u>Kevin's delayed arrival</u> was not delivered.

35

Name _____ **Prepositions**

Prepositional Phrases as Adjectives and Adverbs

A **prepositional phrase** functions like an adjective when it describes a noun in a sentence. A prepositional phrase functions like an adverb when it modifies a verb in a sentence.

Examples:
The police hurried <u>*to the scene*</u>. (prepositional phrase as adverb)
The girl <u>*in pink*</u> is my older sister. (prepositional phrase as adjective)

Underline the prepositional phrase in each sentence. Fill in the blank with adjective (ADJ) or adverb (ADV) as appropriate.

<u>ADV</u> 1. A caterpillar crawled <u>up the stalk</u>.

<u>ADJ</u> 2. The train <u>to Nuremberg</u> was late.

<u>ADJ</u> 3. The room <u>to the left</u> is the guest bedroom.

<u>ADV</u> 4. Andre fell <u>in the mud puddle</u>.

<u>ADV</u> 5. The mail should arrive <u>at two o'clock</u>.

<u>ADV</u> 6. The key is <u>in my purse</u>.

<u>ADJ</u> 7. He ate a piece <u>of my cookie</u>.

<u>ADV</u> 8. Fabienne hid <u>behind the palm tree</u>.

<u>ADV</u> 9. Who is the woman <u>with the red hair</u>?

<u>ADJ</u> 10. The flowers <u>on the back porch</u> need watering.

<u>ADV</u> 11. My sister works <u>in the Central Business District</u>.

<u>ADV</u> 12. It will undoubtedly rain <u>before morning</u>.

<u>ADJ</u> 13. I bought a car <u>with a sun roof</u>.

<u>ADV</u> 14. The ferry <u>to Giglio</u> sails hourly.

<u>ADJ</u> 15. This pottery is <u>from the Yucatan Peninsula</u>.

36

107

Answer Key

Name _____ Prepositions

Changing Prepositional Phrases

Underline the prepositional phrase in each sentence. Rewrite the sentence changing the prepositional phrase to a possessive noun.

Example: The cost *of the ticket* seemed excessive.
          The ticket's cost seemed excessive.

1. The reunion *of the sisters* was a tearjerker.
   The sisters' reunion was a tearjerker.
2. The ending *of the novel* was a big disappointment.
   The novel's ending was a big disappointment.
3. The intentions *of Carmen* are very clear.
   Carmen's intentions are very clear.
4. The weight *of her suitcase* was incredible.
   Her suitcase's weight was incredible.
5. The recipe *of Josephine* makes the absolute best oyster dressing.
   Josephine's recipe makes the absolute best oyster dressing.
6. Mr. Travis lived the life *of a hermit*.
   Mr. Travis lived a hermit's life.
7. The performance *of the diva* was a big disappointment.
   The diva's performance was a big disappointment.
8. The actions *of Stephanie* were heartless.
   Stephanie's actions were heartless.
9. The portrait *of Tim* was an oil painting.
   Tim's portrait was an oil painting.
10. The pet *of the teacher* could not win a popularity contest.
    The teacher's pet could not win a popularity contest.

Name _____ Prepositions

Prepositional Phrases

Change the following phrases consisting of a noun and its modifiers to a prepositional phrase describing the noun.

Example: a jungle animal
          an animal *of the jungle*

1. the Swahili language   the language of the Swahili
2. the cheerleading squad   the squad for cheerleading
3. the precipice's edge   the edge of the precipice
4. the flawed account   the account with a flaw
5. the unexpected discovery   the discovery of the unexpected
6. the garden path   the path through the garden
7. the painful look   the look of pain
8. the freckled nose   the nose with freckles
9. the mournful sound   the sound of mournfulness
10. the isolated retreat   the retreat in isolation
11. the wrought iron chairs   the chairs of wrought iron
12. the Chilean flag   the flag of Chili
13. the red-haired woman   the woman with the red hair
14. the intensely hot summer   the summer of intense heat
15. the renowned playwright   the playwright of renown

Name _____ Conjunctions

Coordinating Conjunctions

Conjunctions join words or groups of words. One kind of conjunction is a coordinating conjunction. **Coordinating conjunctions** connect single words, phrases, and clauses that are of the same importance or rank. The most common coordinating conjunctions are *and, but, or, nor, yet, for,* and *so*. *Nor* is only used in negative sentences.
Examples: The children feasted on cookies *and* milk. (joins words)
           The kids asked me to come *and* join them. (joins phrases)
           I can go, *but* you can't. (joins clauses or simple sentences)
           Roses need drainage, *or* their leaves turn yellow. (joins clauses)
           I never eat fast food *nor* candy. (joins words)

Read each sentence. Supply an appropriate coordinating conjunction. Write on the line if it is joining words (W), phrases (P), or clauses (C).

C 1. There are two trails in the rain forest, __so__ hikers can choose a short or long walk.
P 2. I intellectually agree __but__ emotionally disagree with your decision.
W 3. The child never sees movies rated PG-13 __or__ R.
W 4. The work was hard __and__ satisfying.
P 5. The lights were dimmed __and__ the play began.
C 6. I must buy this painting, __for__ it will look terrific in my living room.
W 7. Will you attend the party given by Melba __and__ Mable?
P 8. Did you finish your homework __or__ did you fall asleep?
P 9. The child can ride the bike __but__ not climb the tree.
W 10. Sloths __and__ iguanas abound in Costa Rica.

Name _____ Conjunctions

Correlative Conjunctions

Conjunctions join words or groups of words. **Correlative conjunctions** are paired connective words that link single words, phrases (combinations of words that go together within sentences), and clauses (word combinations containing subjects and predicates). The correlative conjunctions are:
           both .... and   neither ... nor   whether .... or
           either .... or   not only ... but (also)

Example: She has met *neither* Polly *nor* Renee. (joins words)
          She can prepare *either* an outline *or* an overview. (joins phrases)
          I don't know *whether* Peter will go *or* Jack will. (joins clauses)

Read each sentence and write the appropriate correlative conjunctions in the blanks provided. Write W in the blank if the correlative conjunctions join words, P for phrases, or C for clauses.

P 1. He __both__ documents everything, __and__ keeps copies.
W 2. He eats __either__ fish __or__ chicken.
P 3. A healthy lifestyle includes __not only__ a good diet __but also__ a regular exercise routine.
W 4. __Neither__ fat __nor__ sugar should appear so regularly in your lunch box.
P 5. __Neither__ the fierce wind __nor__ the relentless rain damaged his property.
W 6. __Either__ October __or__ March is the best time to visit Europe.
P 7. __Neither__ the regional tourist office __nor__ the tour operator had the information we requested.
C 8. __Either__ get off the phone now, __or__ you will not use it the rest of the week.

Answer Key

Page 41

Name _____   Conjunctions

Subordinating Conjunctions

Conjunctions join words, phrases, or clauses. **Subordinating conjunctions** join subordinate (dependent) clauses to main (independent clauses). Subordinate clauses contain a subject and predicate, but do not stand alone as a complete thought. Main clauses can stand alone. Subordinating conjunctions clarify meaning about time, possibility, comparison, location, and cause and effect. Common subordinating conjunctions include: *after, as, before, once, till, until, when, whenever, while, as if, as though, if, unless, whether, although, than, though, how, where, wherever, because, since, whereas,* and *why.*

Examples: <u>When</u> you get here, we will begin immediately. (time)
<u>If</u> you do not call him by tonight, you will miss your chance. (possibility)
<u>Although</u> they look similar, ravens and crows are different. (comparison)
I will follow you <u>wherever</u> you go. (location)
<u>Because</u> rain was threatening, we postponed the barbecue. (cause/effect)

Read the two simple sentences. Make them into one sentence by adding a subordinating conjunction to the sentence.

Example: He saw her. He fell in love.
When he saw her, he fell in love.

1. I whistle. I work.

   I whistle while I work.

2. No records were kept. No evidence remains.

   Since no records were kept, no evidence remains.

3. Mary had her first swimming lesson. She became more confident.

   After Mary had her first swimming lesson, she became more confident.

4. The howler monkey was timid. He took the banana from my hand.

   Although the howler monkey was timid, he took the banana from my hand.

5. Elaine walks her dog. All the dogs in the neighborhood bark.

   When Elaine walks her dog, all the dogs in the neighborhood bark.

6. It is summer time. The grass grows faster.

   While it is summer time, the grass grows faster.

© Carson Dellosa CD-3745   41

Page 42

Name _____   Conjunctions

Subordinating Conjunctions

Read the two simple sentences. Make them into one sentence by adding a subordinating conjunction to the sentence.

Examples:
Tourists go to Costa Rica to see the Arenal Volcano. It often has small eruptions.
<u>Tourists go to Costa Rica to see the Arenal Volcano *because* it often has small eruptions.</u>
Rhoda was gone. Her rival took advantage of the situation.
<u>*While* Rhoda was gone, her rival took advantage of the situation.</u>

1. Rita did not get the lead. She chose not to be in the play.

   After Rita did not get the lead, she chose not to be in the play.

2. Valerie couldn't go. Jim didn't want to go.

   Because Valerie couldn't go, Jim didn't want to go.

3. We'll postpone our trip to Hong Kong. We will have more spending money.

   We'll postpone our trip to Hong Kong until we have more spending money.

4. Peggy was prettier. Dottie had a better personality.

   Although Peggy was prettier, Dottie had a better personality.

5. The runner-up can become Miss America. The winner abdicates the throne.

   The runner-up can become Miss America if the winner abdicates the throne.

6. Give me some of your cookies. I'll give you some of my popcorn.

   If you give me some of your cookies, I'll give you some of my popcorn.

7. Janet will talk to Jim. He must apologize.

   Before Janet will talk to Jim, he must apologize.

8. We are going to New England. The leaves change.

   We are going to New England when the leaves change.

© Carson Dellosa CD-3745   42

Page 43

Name _____   Interjections

Interjections

Interjections express some emotion, but have no grammatical connection to the sentence. They can be followed by a comma or an exclamation point. Some commonly used interjections include: *Oh, Darn, Great, Aha, Wow, Ouch, Yech, Shh, Hey,* and *Whew.*

Example: <u>Oh</u>, so there you are!
<u>Darn</u>! I left my umbrella at home.

Add an interjection to each sentence.

1. _Ouch_ ! That really hurts.
2. _Hey_ , I got an A on the exam!
3. _Oh_ , I see.
4. _Wow_ , we have enough money to buy the VCR.
5. _Yech_ ! I hate broccoli.
6. _Hey_ , watch where you're going!
7. _Wow_ , it's so hot.
8. _Wow_ , you look terrific in that dress!
9. _Shh_ ! The teacher is coming.
10. _Great_ , the sky is falling!
11. _Oh_ ! Do you expect me to believe that?
12. _Great_ , I get it.
13. _Aha_ , there's a steep drop here.
14. _Great_ , I've finally finished.
15. _Hey_ ! It's raining again.

© Carson Dellosa CD-3745   43

Page 44

Name _____   Parts of Speech

Review

Identify the underlined part of speech in each sentence. These include noun (N), pronoun (PRO), verb (V), adjective (ADJ), adverb (ADV), conjunction (C), preposition (PRE), and interjection (INT).

<u>PRE</u> 1. *Les Miserables* was written <u>by</u> Victor Hugo.

<u>N</u> 2. Hugo was an influential writer in France in the nineteenth <u>century</u>.

<u>PRO</u> 3. Judith, have <u>you</u> seen *Les Miserables* on Broadway or in London?

<u>V</u> 4. Jean Valjean <u>is</u> the protagonist.

<u>ADJ</u> 5. Do you consider Javert or Thernardier to be the <u>real</u> villain?

<u>C</u> 6. Jean Valjean went to prison for a total of nineteen years <u>because</u> he stole a loaf of bread and then tried to escape from prison.

<u>N</u> 7. Mayor Madeleine was an <u>alias</u> for Jean Valjean.

<u>PRE</u> 8. Javert pursued Jean Valjean <u>with</u> a vengeance.

<u>ADV</u> 9. Thernardier bargained <u>craftily</u> to make a dishonest profit.

<u>N</u> 10. Marius exhibited great <u>loyalty</u> to the revolutionaries in the novel.

<u>ADV</u> 11. Marius and Cosette fell <u>madly</u> in love.

<u>ADJ</u> 12. Eponine felt <u>unrequited</u> love for Marius.

<u>C</u> 13. Azelma and Eponine were treated well by their mother, <u>but</u> Gavroche was not.

<u>ADV</u> 14. The bishop was the <u>most</u> influential person in Valjean's life.

<u>PRE</u> 15. Cosette spent <u>about</u> five years in a convent school in Paris.

<u>ADV</u> 16. Cosette and Valjean <u>often</u> strolled in the Luxembourg Gardens in the spring.

© Carson Dellosa CD-3745   44

Answer Key

Name _____ Sentence Patterns

Subject Verb (S-V)

Most sentences belong to one of five basic types. The simplest consists of a noun, pronoun, or noun phrase serving as the **subject, followed by a verb** (SV). Modifiers add information or interest to the sentence pattern without changing it.

Examples: Babies sleep. (S-V)
                The tiny babies sleep blissfully in their sturdy cribs. (S-V)

Read each sentence. Write SV if the sentence fits this pattern. Underline the subject once and the verb twice. Write *no* if the sentence does not have the SV pattern.

_SV_ 1. The tall girl in the red dress left early.

_SV_ 2. We took the latest flight to Pensacola on Friday afternoon.

_SV_ 3. The dictionary sat on the desk.

_SV_ 4. The band played in the afternoon.

_SV_ 5. The plane landed.

_SV_ 6. Show me.

_SV_ 7. The approaching train blew its whistle.

_SV_ 8. The naughty pup hid in the bushes.

_SV_ 9. Rebecca and I quarreled.

_SV_ 10. We drove to the Pacific Coast.

_SV_ 11. We rented a cottage on the beach.

_SV_ 12. Margaret arrived at noon.

_SV_ 13. Our club meets on Tuesday night.

_SV_ 14. I bought a souvenir for the babysitter.

© Carson Dellosa CD-3745   45

Name _____ Sentence Patterns

Subject, Verb, and Object (S-V-O)

In the S-V-O sentence pattern, a direct object follows the verb. It names the person or thing directly acted on by the action described by the verb. It answers the question Who or What after the action verb. Modifiers (adjectives, adverbs, and prepositional phrases) do not affect the sentence pattern.

	S	V	DO
Examples:	*Robert*	met	*Elizabeth.*
	Robert	ate	*cookies.*
	Robert	knew	*them.*
	Sly Robert	knew	*details* of the twisted plot.

Read each sentence. Write SVO if the sentence fits this pattern. Underline the subject once, the verb twice and circle the direct object. Write *no* if it does not fit the SVO pattern.

SVO 1. Zachary gave the (money) to Charles.

SVO 2. Ralph sharpened his (pencil) before class.

_no_ 3. The dollar fell under the table.

SVO 4. Ed mowed the (grass) in the backyard.

SVO 5. Monica concocts her own (facial) of cucumbers and honey.

SVO 6. Carla found a five dollar (bill) in the street.

_no_ 7. After the battle, most of the enemy surrendered.

SVO 8. Fagin and Bill Sykes kidnapped (Oliver Twist) in the novel by Dickens.

SVO 9. Mrs. Blanchard frequently called daytime talk (shows.)

_no_ 10. Benny took his sister's (ice cream) and ate it.

_no_ 11. Evelyn rests in the afternoon after work.

SVO 12. Albert burned his (hand) on the grill of the barbecue pitt.

© Carson Dellosa CD-3745   46

Name _____ Sentence Patterns

Subject, Verb, Indirect Object, Direct Object (S-V-IO-DO)

In the S-V-IO-DO sentence pattern, an indirect object tells to whom or for whom a direct object is intended. It immediately follows the verb and is followed by the direct object. Modifiers (adjectives, adverbs, and prepositional phrases) do not affect the sentence pattern.

	S	V	IO	DO
Examples:	*Patty*	gave	*Sharon*	a *present.*
	Patty	gave	*her*	a *present.*
	Patty	gave	*young Sharon*	a *present.*

Read each sentence. Write *yes* in the blank if the sentence fits the S-V-IO-DO pattern. Divide the sentence into subject (S), verb (V), direct object (DO), and indirect object (IO). Write *no*, if the sentence does not fit this pattern. The first one has been done for you.

yes 1. Lee / gave / Dave / a fax machine for Christmas.
         S   V   IO   DO

yes 2. Evelyn / told / her mother / a lie.
         S   V   IO   DO

_no_ 3. Martha left her purse in the car.

yes 4. The unscrupulous man / sold / the elderly couple / some worthless land.
             S   V   IO   DO

_no_ 5. Her mother sent a birthday box to Meghan at camp.

_no_ 6. Chris sent her daughter to Europe as a graduation present.

yes 7. Lynette / gave / the fuzzy puppy / a big hug.
        S   V   IO   DO

yes 8. Mr. Ullrich / left / Malcolm / a big project for the weekend.
        S   V   IO   DO

yes 9. The tutor / gave / Steven / some much-needed help in math.
        S   V   IO   DO

_no_ 10. Marianne writes to her penpal frequently.

yes 11. Blake / bought / his colleague / a cup of coffee.
        S   V   IO   DO

_no_ 12. Roger drives his sister to school on Tuesday.

© Carson Dellosa CD-3745   47

Name _____ Sentence Patterns

Subject, Verb, Direct Object, Object Compliment (S-V-DO-OC)

In the S-V-DO-OC pattern, a noun or adjective called an object complement, identifies or describes the direct object. The object complement follows the direct object.

	S	V	DO	OC
Examples:	*Alyssa*	found	the *movie*	amusing.
	Kim	named	her *daughter*	Allison.

Read each sentence. Write *yes* in the blank if the sentence fits the S-V-DO-OC pattern. Divide the sentence into subject (S), verb (V), direct object (DO), and object complement(OC). Write *no*, if the sentence does not fit this pattern.

yes 1. The hurricane / made / our sliding glass door / dangerous.
        S   V   DO   OC

yes 2. Mrs. Bell / considered / the children / foolish.
        S   V   DO   OC

_no_ 3. We saw the president during the White House tour.
        S V

_no_ 4. The elderly woman / was declared / incompetent by her heirs.

_no_ 5. The deer gave the hunter a good chase.
        S   V

yes 6. The judges / declared / my sister / Miss Teenage America.
        S   V   DO   OC

yes 7. The critic / called / the movie / a flop.
        S   V   DO OC

yes 8. We / painted / the trim / bright white.
        S   V   DO OC

yes 9. The new interstate entrance / makes / downtown / convenient.
        S   V   DO   OC

yes 10. The neighborhood / found / the farm animals / objectionable.
        S   V   DO   OC

yes 11. The students / found / the new jazz group / very innovative.
        S   V   DO   OC

yes 12. The class / elected / Marvin / treasurer.
        S   V   DO   OC

yes 13. The explanation of iambic pentameter / was making / Dorothy / sleepy.
             S   V   DO OC

yes 14. Her high blood pressure / made / her condition / worse.
          S   V   DO   OC

© Carson Dellosa CD-3745   48

Answer Key

Name _____

Sentence Patterns

Subject, Linking Verb, and Predicate Adjective (S-LV-PA)

In the Subject-Linking Verb-Predicate Adjective (S-LV-PA) pattern, the subject is followed by a linking verb. The linking verb describes conditions, not actions, and connects the subject with adjectives that follow it. In addition to forms of the verb *to be* and *become*, other common linking verbs used in S-LV-PA patterns include *seem, become, appear, look, taste, feel, smell, sound, stay, grow,* and *remain.*

Example:
S   LV   PA
His *date*   *became*   *bored* with the subject.

Read the sentence. Write *yes* if the sentence follows the S-LV-PA pattern. Divide the sentence into subject (S), linking verb (V), and predicate adjective (PA). Write *no*, if the sentence does not fit this pattern.

___yes___ 1. Jane's new watch / looks / expensive.
                    S   V   PA

___yes___ 2. The house / appeared / adequate for such a large family.
                  S   V   PA

___no___ 3. I / found / the heat / unbearable.
                S   V   DO   OC

___yes___ 4. Marie's stomach / felt / terrible after lunch.
                     S   V   PA

___no___ 5. Audrey Hepburn / was / a very talented actress.
                     S   V   PN

___yes___ 6. Fred Astaire's dancing / was / memorable.
                        S   V   PA

___yes___ 7. Maggie / was / sad about her grade on the essay.
                  S   V   PA

___yes___ 8. Willard / grew / sleepy during the long lecture.
                 S   V   PA

___yes___ 9. Sally / seemed / uncomfortable around Matthew.
                 S   V   PA

___yes___ 10. Ms. Davis / is / the leader in the polls.
                    S   V   PN

___yes___ 11. The street / was / too noisy on the weekends.
                     S   V   PA

___yes___ 12. The faculty / felt / hostile towards the inflexible new principal.
                     S   V   PA

49

Name _____

Sentence Patterns

Subject, Linking Verb, and Predicate Nominative (S-LV-PN)

In the S-LV-PN pattern, what follows the linking verb renames the subject. The linking verb describes conditions, not actions. Forms of the verb *to be* (am, is, are, was, and were) are the most common linking verbs. Another common linking verb used in this sentence pattern is *to become.* Modifiers (adjectives, adverbs and prepositional phrases) do not affect the sentence pattern.

Example:
                    S   LV   PN
My favorite *snack*   *is*   chocolate *cake.*

Notice that this sentence can be reversed, so that the predicate nominative becomes the subject and vice versa.

Example:
                 S   LV   PN
Chocolate *cake*   *is*   my favorite *snack.*

Read each sentence. If the pattern is S-LV-PN, write *yes* in the blank and rewrite the sentence so that the PN becomes the subject. If the sentence is not in this pattern, write *no*.

___yes___ 1. An <u>orange</u> is a good (source) of vitamin C.

A good source of vitamin C is an orange.

___yes___ 2. <u>Computerization</u> is the (solution) to their antiquated system.

The solution to their antiquated system is computerization.

___no___ 3. This credit <u>card</u> <u>charges</u> no annual (fee.)
_____

___yes___ 4. <u>Julie Andrews</u> is a dearly-beloved (singer.)

A dearly-beloved singer is Julie Andrews.

___no___ 5. <u>Jody</u> <u>was</u> (delighted) to find money in her pocket.
_____

___yes___ 6. The <u>man</u> in the Hawaiian shirt <u>is</u> my (doctor.)

My doctor is the man in the Hawaiian shirt.

50

Name _____

Sentence Patterns

Noun Function in Sentence Patterns

Read the following sentences. Each contains an underlined noun. Determine the function of the noun in each sentence. Decide between subject (S), direct object (DO), object complement (OC), predicate nominative (PN). Write the function in the blank provided.

_PN_ 1. Louisa May Alcott was the <u>author</u> of *Little Women.*

_DO_ 2. Alcott wrote many successful <u>novels.</u>

_S_ 3. Her spunky <u>heroine</u> Jo is a great favorite with young readers.

_S_ 4. Jo's <u>dream</u> was to become a published writer.

_S_ 5. Her <u>talent</u> flourished under the guidance of Professor Baer.

_PN_ 6. Amy was Jo's <u>sister.</u>

_DO_ 7. Amy destroyed Jo's precious <u>manuscript</u> in retaliation for a sisterly squabble.

_OP_ 8. This incident made Jo <u>angry.</u>

_DO_ 9. Jo felt no <u>jealousy</u> toward Amy when Amy eventually married Laurie.

_DO_ 10. Jo had the closest <u>relationship</u> with her sister Beth.

_S_ 11. The <u>death</u> of Beth is one of the most poignant episodes in the novel.

_S_ 12. Beth's selfless <u>life</u> contributed to her untimely death.

_DO_ 13. Jo had many good <u>times</u> with her older sister Meg.

_DO_ 14. Although Jo felt uncomfortable at dances, Meg loved the elegance and <u>gaiety.</u>

51

Name _____

Sentence Patterns

Sentence Pattern Review

Read the following sentences. Each contains the noun *sister.* Determine the function of *sister* in each sentence. Label the function as one of the following:

S—subject   DO—direct object
OC—object complement   IO—indirect object
PN—predicate nominative

_PN_ 1. Amy March is Meg March's youngest <u>sister.</u>

_OC_ 2. Mrs. Laurence and Laurie considered each other <u>sisters.</u>

_S_ 3. Although Beth survived rheumatic fever, this <u>sister</u> would never regain her health.

_IO_ 4. Meg gave her <u>sister</u> Amy some money to buy limes.

_DO_ 5. To everyone's surprise, Laurie married the youngest <u>sister</u> instead of Jo.

_PN_ 6. Jo is the <u>sister</u> who is definitely the central character.

_DO_ 7. Aunt March showed obvious partiality to the youngest <u>sister.</u>

_PN_ 8. Meg was the oldest <u>sister</u> in the March family as well as the prettiest.

_S_ 9. The <u>sister</u> most involved in acts of charity was gentle Beth.

_IO_ 10. Mr. Laurence gave Beth a piano because he was particularly fond of this <u>sister.</u>

Use the noun *school* in any three of the functions listed above.

1. _S—My school is the best school._

2. _OP—He took me to school._

3. _IO—Mr. Smith gave the school a donation._

52

Answer Key

Name _____ Sentence Types

Simple Sentence

A **simple sentence** consists of a single independent clause or complete thought. It can have more than one subject, and more than one verb and still be a simple sentence. It can be lengthened by adding modifiers and complements.

Examples: The vase fell. (one subject, one verb)
The vase and statue fell. (two subjects, one verb)
The vase fell and broke. (one subject, two verbs)
The vase and statue fell and broke. (two subjects, two verbs)
The fragile vase fell off the dresser and completely shattered. (one subject, two verbs, many modifiers)

Write S if the sentence is simple. Write *no* if it is not simple.

_S_ 1. Madeline hungrily ate grapes at the table.

_S_ 2. Jack and Elizabeth drank milk out of the carton.

_S_ 3. Roger is the distinguished man in the dark blue suit.

_NO_ 4. Roger, who is a noted inventor, is working on a secret project.

_S_ 5. The girl looked in the mirror and combed her pretty hair.

_S_ 6. The ghost appears in the hall every night and terrorizes the guests.

_NO_ 7. Drew yawned and stretched, but he could not get out of bed.

_S_ 8. Sharon paints landscapes well.

_no_ 9. We all knew who was in trouble.

_S_ 10. The outfielders were missing easy fly balls.

_no_ 11. Gladys was not tired, but her tennis partner was.

_no_ 12. A person who has mastered a second language is bilingual.

© Carson Dellosa CD-3745   53

Name _____ Sentence Types

Compound Sentences

A **compound sentence** contains two or more independent clauses. The coordinating conjunction (*and, but, so, or, nor* or *yet*) that joins the two independent clauses suggests that the two clauses are equally important. A comma usually precedes the coordinating conjunction, but may be omitted if the first clause is short. A semicolon can take the place of the coordinating conjunction.

Examples: Most of the girls favored the suggestion, but the boys did not.
Most of the girls favored the suggestion; the boys did not.
That was fun but now we must go home.

Write CMP if the sentence is compound or NO if it is not compound.

CMP 1. The weather was perfect, and everyone eagerly anticipated the outing.

_NO_ 2. The cat chased the mouse which had eluded him for days.

CMP 3. Liza sang ten songs, but the audience clamored for more.

CMP 4. He spotted the horse, but it quickly galloped away.

_NO_ 5. Glenda played basketball and won a sports scholarship.

CMP 6. A strange dog chased us, but his owner came to our rescue.

CMP 7. Ruby bought the blouse, and the brooch was given to her.

CMP 8. She labeled Jack foolhardy, and she pronounced Jill foolish.

_NO_ 9. The writer got discouraged when he had been rejected three times.

CMP 10. I brought cash, but it wasn't enough.

CMP 11. The airfare was cheap, so Marva bought the ticket.

_NO_ 12. *The 60's* by Blake Bailey is informative and entertaining.

© Carson Dellosa CD-3745   54

Name _____ Sentence Types

Complex Sentences

A **complex sentence** contains one independent clause and one or more dependent clauses. The independent clause is the more important of the two, and the dependent clause modifies it in some way. A clause introduced by a subordinating conjunction can appear within the independent clause as well as before or after it.

Examples: When we saw the repair estimate, we decided to buy a new car.
We didn't think we could afford a new car, until we saw the cost of repairs.
Because the cost of repairs was so high, we bought a new car.
The girl sitting in the front who is driving the red convertible is my sister.

Write CPX if the sentence is complex. Underline the independent clause once and underline the dependent clause(s) twice. Write *no* if the sentence is not complex.

CPX 1. The roof leaks whenever it rains.

CPX 2. I told the ophthalmologist that I was seeing double since I got my new glasses.

CPX 3. Because the city faces a huge deficit, a new tax has been proposed.

CPX 4. Lauren told me that the idea was hers because she thought of it first.

CPX 5. When a player spikes the volleyball, he hits it sharply downward.

CPX 6. Charles is a perfectionist who rarely fails to spot an error.

CPX 7. The nickel has diminished in value since it can no longer buy a telephone call.

CPX 8. The dog barks incessantly whenever the mailman comes.

_NO_ 9. Venice is accessible by boat or foot, but not by car.

CPX 10. Avery is one of those kids who always scores high on tests.

CPX 11. Whenever Vincent thinks of Vanessa who is his girlfriend, he smiles.

_NO_ 12. The artist painted lovely Venetian scenes in watercolor.

© Carson Dellosa CD-3745   55

Name _____ Sentence Types

Compound-Complex Sentences

Compound-Complex sentences combine two (or more) independent clauses and at least one dependent clause.

Example: Mark tried to do the algebra homework alone, but he realized that he needed some assistance after he had spent several hours on it.

Write CC if the sentence is compound-complex. Underline the independent clauses once. Underline the dependent clause(s) twice. Write *no* if the sentence is not compound-complex.

_CC_ 1. We use whatever is donated, but we especially welcome toys.

_CC_ 2. The room that Carrie painted had been white, but she changed the color to pale blue.

_no_ 3. You are the person who I want to see.

_CC_ 4. She was going to the beach for the weekend until the tropical storm developed, so she decided to change her plans.

_CC_ 5. The masker who had worn the striking jester costume was in the contest, but he did not win first prize.

_CC_ 6. Although Bill was hesitant to run for mayor, his friends encouraged him, and he entered the race.

_no_ 7. What kind of car do you want to buy?

_CC_ 8. While Valerie was shopping for souvenirs, Michael was snorkeling at the reef, and Monica was taking a guided tour of the island.

_CC_ 9. Colonel Mowry was reading in the study, and Professor Peach was napping in the conservatory, when the murder took place.

_CC_ 10. The wine was superb and the food was excellent although the service was definitely lacking.

© Carson Dellosa CD-3745   56

Answer Key

Name _____ Sentence Types

Review

Rewrite each sentence as directed in the parentheses that follow it. S is simple, CD is compound, CX is complex, and CC is compound-complex.

Example: The dog was barking incessantly, and the cat was crying loudly. (CD to CC)
When the thunderstorm reached its peak, the dog was barking incessantly and the cat was crying loudly.

1. Just as the plane departed, the passenger arrived at the airport. **(CX to CC)**
   Just as the plane departed, the passenger arrived at the airport and she rushed to the gate.

2. The carpet was ruined in the flood, and the chairs were damaged. **(CD to CX)**
   The carpet was ruined in the flood when the furniture was damaged.

3. The electricity went out during the storm. **(S to CD)**
   The electricity went out during the storm, but it was restored shortly.

4. The fax machine ran out of paper. **(S to CX)**
   When we tried to receive the document, the fax machine ran out of paper.

5. There was broken glass everywhere, and I didn't have a broom. **(CD to CC)**
   After the shelf fell, there was broken glass everywhere and I didn't have a broom.

6. After I let the cake cool, I iced it with fudge frosting. **(CX to CD)**
   I let the cake cool, and I iced it with fudge frosting.

© Carson Dellosa CD-3745   57

Name _____ Sentence Types

Review

Classify each of the following sentences as one of the following:

S) Simple **CD)** Compound **CX)** Complex **CC)** Compound Complex

CX 1. If you do not help me, I will fail the course.
S 2. I have investigated the new building project thoroughly.
CD 3. Marcia lives in Houston, but her brother John lives here.
CX 4. Since we have begun this discussion, you have refused to listen.
CX 5. If he changes his mind, order him to leave.
CX 6. A woman, who was wearing a big hat, sat in front of me at the movies.
CD 7. Sue lectured the first hour, and we asked questions the second hour.
CD 8. My brother is good at water skiing, but he is a dunce at snow skiing.
CX 9. Although you are a friend, I must disapprove of your actions.
CX 10. Margaret refused because she had other plans.
CX 11. Everyone always laughs when Arthur sneezes.
CD 12. Dianna waited patiently, but the bus never came.
CC 13. I am sure that James does not know what danger is involved, and he will get in trouble.
CX 14. Behind the church was a path that led to the cemetery.
CC 15. The telephone rang twice, and Stevie, who was closest, answered it.
CX 16. Uncle Elton arrived after everyone had gone to bed.

© Carson Dellosa CD-3745   58

Name _____ Sentence Types

Review

Classify each of the following sentences as one of the following:

S) Simple **CD)** Compound **CX)** Complex **CC)** Compound Complex

CD 1. Matt can do a triple flip, and Kathy can do a double flip.
CX 2. Since I joined the speech club, I have had more self-confidence.
CX 3. Jim Thomas, who lives next door, is going to camp in July.
CD 4. The spokes are broken, and the frame is rusty and bent.
CX 5. If you want to arrive on time, listen carefully to the directions.
S 6. Flights to Dallas, Los Angeles, and San Francisco leave in ten minutes.
S 7. I need a major overhaul on my bicycle.
CD 8. Dad washes the dishes, and Mom mows the lawn.
CC 9. My mother was wrong this time, and I told her that I did not agree.
CX 10. I think that I am the smartest kid around.
CX 11. Anyone who is a member may bring a guest.
S 12. Sara enjoys the company of small children.
CX 13. We all knew the one who had received top honors in math.
S 14. Cypress was first settled by the Greeks.
CD 15. You must abide by the rules of the contract, or you will lose your job.
S 16. Louise is the best biologist in the laboratory.
CX 17. Because we were so late, we called a taxi.
S 18. Mark read the story and laughed to himself.

© Carson Dellosa CD-3745   59

Name _____ Verbals

Gerunds

A **gerund** is a verb form used as a noun. It uses the *-ing* verb ending. Like verbs, gerunds name actions or conditions. Like nouns, gerunds function in sentences as subjects (**S**), direct objects (**DO**), predicate nominatives (**PN**), or objects of prepositions (**OP**). A gerund can stand alone, or it can be part of a gerund phrase.

Examples: Dame Van Winkle's nagging made Rip's life miserable. (gerund as **S**)
Rip Van Winkle hated his wife's nagging. (gerund as **DO**)
The cause of Rip's discontent was his wife's nagging. (gerund as **PN**)
Rip's life from the constant nagging was unbearable. (gerund as **OP**)

Underline the gerund in each of the following sentences.

1. The driver was fined for littering on the highway.
2. He found running for office to be a grueling experience.
3. Smoking was ruining his health.
4. Reading was a challenging activity to the six year old.
5. Eating homemade ice cream was the ruination of her diet.
6. Packing for summer camp took Meghan all weekend.

Underline the gerund. Classify its function in the sentence from the following: S, DO, PN, or OP. If there is no gerund in the sentence, write NONE.

S 1. Playing tennis is great aerobic exercise.
DO 2. The teacher loved singing as a way to unwind.
PN 3. The object of the game was winning.
OP 4. He bought those new shoes for golfing.
S 5. Marrying him is her goal.

© Carson Dellosa CD-3745   60

Answer Key

Name _____ Verbals

Participles

A participle is a verb form used as an adjective.

Examples: Drew had a flat-bottomed <u>fishing</u> boat.
             I sat in the <u>broken</u> chair.

Look at the underlined word in each sentence. Write V if the underlined word functions as a verb. Write P if it functions as a participle (verbal).

_V_ 1. My former English teacher is <u>running</u> for public office.

_P_ 2. I forgot my <u>running</u> shoes.

_P_ 3. The <u>dented</u> fender was an unpleasant surprise.

_V_ 4. Someone just <u>dented</u> the bumper of my car.

_V_ 5. My neighbors will soon be <u>moving</u>.

_P_ 6. They'll need to rent a <u>moving</u> van.

_P_ 7. The <u>misplaced</u> memo caused big problems.

_V_ 8. Whom do you think <u>misplaced</u> the memo?

_P_ 9. I hope that I have an <u>experienced</u> pilot on this flight.

_V_ 10. I <u>experienced</u> air sickness from the turbulence.

_P_ 11. Molly was surprised to learn that an oyster is a <u>living</u> creature.

_P_ 12. The <u>living</u> conditions in the tenement were not acceptable.

_V_ 13. Carmen is <u>chilling</u> the champagne.

_P_ 14. A <u>chilling</u> tale was told around the campfire.

_P_ 15. The <u>proposed</u> amendment was very controversial.

Name _____ Verbals

Gerund and Participle Review

Look at each underlined word. Classify it as one of the following: gerund (G), participle (P), or verb (V).

_V_ 1. The detective is <u>investigating</u> a domestic matter.

_P_ 2. The <u>investigating</u> officer was called to the stand.

_G_ 3. By <u>investigating</u>, I was able to find the answer.

_G_ 4. Morton especially loves <u>skiing</u> in Bornio.

_V_ 5. The advanced students are <u>skiing</u> on a different slope.

_P_ 6. The <u>skiing</u> instructor was from Utah.

_G_ 7. <u>Participating</u> in the dangerous rescue attempt was heroic.

_V_ 8. All of the local high schools are <u>participating</u> in the speech tournament.

_P_ 9. Get your free gift at all <u>participating</u> stores.

_G_ 10. Claudia enjoys <u>volunteering</u> at Children's Hospital.

_V_ 11. Jana is <u>volunteering</u> her time at a homeless shelter.

_V_ 12. Are you <u>volunteering</u> to help?

_V_ 13. Anis is <u>reading</u> a new Stephan King novel.

_P_ 14. Mrs. Cunningham is her <u>reading</u> teacher.

_G_ 15. Roxanna enjoys <u>reading</u> more than any other activity.

_G_ 16. <u>Flying</u> to Hong Kong is very expensive.

_V_ 17. I am <u>flying</u> to Hong Kong in November.

_P_ 18. Carlo took <u>flying</u> lessons when he was twenty.

Name _____ Verbals

Infinitives as Nouns

Infinitives are verb forms preceded by the word *to*. They can be used in sentences as nouns, adjectives, or adverbs. When **infinitives function as nouns**, they can be used as subjects (S), predicate nominatives (PN), direct objects (DO), or objects of prepositions (OP).

Examples: My choice is <u>to leave</u>. (infinitive as PN)
             <u>To redesign</u> would take a long time. (infinitive as S)
             The child began <u>to cry</u>. (infinitive as DO)
             She did not respond except <u>to glare</u>. (infinitive as OP)
             I gave a hug to my friend. (no infinitive)

Underline the infinitive in each sentence. Then write S if it is used as a subject DO if it is used as a direct object PN if it is used as a predicate nominative or OP if the infinitive is used as an object of a preposition. If there is no infinitive, write NONE.

_DO_ 1. I just want <u>to finish</u>.

_PN_ 2. Her passion is <u>to dance</u>.

_S_ 3. <u>To walk</u> is good exercise.

NONE 4. I will walk to the mall.

_DO_ 5. My penmanship needs <u>to improve</u>.

_DO_ 6. Our maid refuses <u>to iron</u>.

NONE 7. I gave a pass to Patrick.

_S_ 8. <u>To escape</u> was impossible.

_S_ 9. <u>To believe</u> is very difficult in this instance.

_OP_ 10. He has nothing on his mind right now except <u>to sleep</u>.

_DO_ 11. I want <u>to look</u>, but it's too scary.

_S_ 12. <u>To win</u> is our goal.

Name _____ Verbals

Infinitives as Adjectives and Adverbs

An infinitive may be used as an adjective when it directly modifies a noun or pronoun in a sentence. It may also be used as an adverb when it directly modifies a verb, adjective, or adverb in the sentence.

Examples: Clara likes chocolate milk <u>to drink</u>. (infinitive as adjective)
             They were disappointed <u>to leave</u>. (infinitive as adverb)

Underline the infinitive in each sentence. Classify it as one of the following: (ADJ) adjective or (ADV) adverb.

ADJ 1. She is a person <u>to admire</u>.

ADJ 2. This watch is the best one <u>to buy</u>.

ADJ 3. I have a train <u>to catch</u>.

ADV 4. Molly was too frightened <u>to move</u>.

ADV 5. Ms. Jacobs plays golf <u>to relax</u>.

ADV 6. Kathleen was too tired <u>to study</u>.

ADJ 7. He has a hard face <u>to forget</u>.

ADJ 8. I have promises <u>to keep</u>.

ADV 9. This map is hard <u>to read</u>.

ADV 10. The name of that country is difficult <u>to spell</u>.

ADV 11. This map is easy <u>to read</u>.

ADV 12. The kitten's fur was so soft <u>to touch</u>.

ADV 13. That malicious comment will be hard <u>to forgive</u>.

ADV 14. This math textbook is designed <u>to provide</u> constant review.

ADV 15. A driver who has had many accidents is difficult <u>to insure</u>.

Answer Key

Name _____ Verbals

Infinitive Phrases as Adjectives and Adverbs

An **infinitive phrase** contains an infinitive and any other words (subjects, objects, and modifiers) needed to complete its meaning. **Infinitive phrases** can function as nouns, adjectives, and adverbs in addition to functioning as nouns.

Examples: The counselor told Mrs. Martin that *Reviving Ophelia* was a good book to read from cover to cover. (adjective phrase)

Sam approached the teacher to explain the situation. (adverb phrase)

Underline each infinitive phrase. Identify it as adjective (ADJ) or adverb (ADV).

ADV   1. Your address is easy to remember at any time.

ADV   2. Models use make-up tricks to cover flaws in their appearances.

ADJ   3. The best type of cheese to eat with a red pasta sauce is Romano.

ADV   4. Meghan mostly uses her computer to type essays.

ADJ   5. Alyssa has never been the type to gossip about other students.

ADJ   6. The best time to go to Disney World is in the fall.

ADJ   7. Babysitting is a good way to learn responsibility.

ADV   8. I need a screwdriver to take apart this bookcase.

ADV   9. Brian had a lot of money to spend at the sporting goods store.

ADJ 10. Sylvia was the best singer to audition for the part.

ADJ 11. The commander gave orders to bomb the target.

ADV 12. To prepare for the test, Anthony needs quiet.

© Carson Dellosa CD-3745   65

Name _____ Verbals

Infinitives as Noun Phrases

An infinitive phrase is a group of words consisting of an infinitive and any other words (subjects, objects, and modifiers) needed to complete its meaning. Infinitive phrases can function as a subjects (S), predicate nominatives (PN), direct objects (DO), or objects of prepositions (OP).

Examples: Amy wants to find a new job. (infinitive phrase as DO)
To skate in The Olympics is her dream. (infinitive phrase as S)
Her dream is to skate in the Olympics. (infinitive phrase as PN)
I gave a lecture to the defiant young offender. (no infinitive phrase)

Underline each infinitive phrase and identify it as a subject (S) direct object (DO) or predicate nominative (PN). Write *no* if the sentence contains no infinitive phrase.

DO   1. Mary loves to eat tomatoes from her own garden.

S   2. To dance at Radio City Music Hall is her fantasy.

DO   3. Valerie wants to finish college in four years.

S   4. To finish this project quickly would be a blessing.

DO   5. Mrs. Shaw just wanted to feel better.

OP   6. We are about to see a new invention.

S   7. To read this entire novel is my weekend homework.

no   8. I gave a copy to my cousin Elizabeth.

DO   9. I tried to stop her, but I failed.

DO 10. Does anyone plan to attend the Fourth of July picnic?

S 11. To follow his lead would be a major mistake.

PN 12. Mrs. Matherne's dream is to own her own business.

© Carson Dellosa CD-3745   66

Name _____ Verbals

Split Infinitives

When a word, phrase, or clause comes between the infinitive *to* and the verb that follows, it is called a split infinitive. This generally results in an awkward sentence. Although there are a few exceptions, it is best to move the word or words that split the infinitive to the end of the sentence or some other spot.

Examples: A reliable car does not need to necessarily be expensive. (awkward)
A reliable car does not necessarily need to be expensive. (better)

Read each sentence. Underline the infinitive. Rewrite the sentence so that there is not a split infinitive.

1. The new movie was designed to directly appeal to preteen girls.

The new movie was designed to appeal directly to preteen girls.

2. The child liked to immediately tattle when the opportunity arose.

The child liked to tattle immediately when the opportunity arose.

3. The talkative couple in the theater was asked to finally stop.

The talkative couple in the theater was finally asked to stop.

4. Beth decided to more neatly rewrite her essay.

Beth decided to rewrite her essay more neatly.

5. Everyone was told to as soon as possible vacate the premises.

Everyone was told to vacate the premises as soon as possible.

© Carson Dellosa CD-3745   67

Name _____ Clauses

Independent and Subordinate Clauses

An **independent (or main) clause** contains a subject and a verb and can stand alone as a sentence. A **subordinate (or dependent) clause** contains a subject and verb, but cannot stand alone as a sentence. The subordinate clause clarifies or adds to the meaning of the independent clause that it accompanies.

Examples: If you need help with your homework, I will help you.
The dress that you chose is too expensive.
(the subordinate clauses are underlined.)

Complete each sentence below by adding a subordinate clause or independent clause. In the blank write IND (independent) or SUB (subordinate) to identify the type of clause you wrote.

SUB 1. Since you got a speeding ticket, you can't borrow the car.

IND 2. If you feed that cat, I'll feed the dog.

SUB 3. The girl who is standing in line is my brother's girlfriend.

SUB 4. Since he studied so much, Mark got an A on the exam.

SUB 5. Since you got a speeding ticket who was chosen to be Miss America.

IND 6. Since I couldn't find you, I went home.

SUB 7. I visited an island where there was an active volcano.

SUB 8. Since you don't have a driver's license, I can't go with you.

SUB 9. Since you got a speeding ticket, I'll be home early.

IND 10. If Henry shows up, tell him we went to Mallini's.

© Carson Dellosa CD-3745   68

© Carson-Dellosa CD-3745   115

Answer Key

Name _____ Clauses

Independent and Dependent Clauses

Identify each clause as independent (IN) or dependent (D). Underline the subordinating conjunction or relative pronoun if there is one. No punctuation or capitalization is provided.

IN 1. she wears too much makeup

D 2. <u>since</u> she is under a lot of stress

D 3. <u>until</u> the entire project is complete

IN 4. we were thirty minutes late for the appointment

D 5. <u>because</u> you're afraid

IN 6. they felt more comfortable with me

D 7. <u>if</u> the turkey is not refrigerated

D 8. <u>although</u> the report was in plain view

D 9. <u>which</u> is in demand

D 10. <u>who</u> knows my brother

IN 11. shadows are longer in the winter

IN 12. it is homemade

D 13. <u>when</u> the plant is over watered

IN 14. it was raining

D 15. <u>because</u> good records were not kept

D 16. <u>until</u> the light bulb was invented

D 17. <u>that</u> I wear to church

IN 18. Sal is arachnophobic

Name _____ Clauses

Independent and Subordinate Clauses

An **independent clause** can stand alone as a sentence. A **subordinate or dependent clause** contains a subject and verb, but does not express a complete thought and can't stand alone as a sentence. The subordinate clause must be attached to the independent clause to complete the meaning. Subordinate clauses are begun with a subordinating conjunction such as *although, because, if, since, until,* and *when* or relative pronouns such as *who, which,* and *that.*

Identify each clause as independent (IND) or subordinate (SUB).

SUB 1. although the cookies were low in fat

IND 2. they were still high in calories

IND 3. Jack paid all his bills

SUB 4. after he received a second notice

SUB 5. who wants seats in the first balcony

IND 6. the people must buy their tickets months in advance

IND 7. Mr. Stickney used his car phone to call a tow truck

SUB 8. after his car overheated

IND 9. the icemaker is broken

SUB 10. although the refrigerator is new

IND 11. Marcia wears high heels every day

SUB 12. since she works downtown

SUB 13. until the road construction is completed

IND 14. we have to leave thirty minutes earlier

SUB 15. since you don't have a flashlight

Name _____ Clauses

Adjective Clauses

Adjective clauses modify a noun or pronoun in the independent clause and are introduced by *who, which,* or *that.*

Example: The coach <u>who was hired last week</u> is doing an impressive job.

Complete each sentence with an adjective clause.

1. The woman _____who is in the kitchen_____ is a famous French chef.

2. The person _____who I saw_____ was wearing a white uniform.

3. The rumor _____that she told_____ is totally untrue.

4. The family _____who lives next door_____ is from Costa Rica.

5. He is the thief _____who I identified_____.

6. The purse _____that was in the window_____ was an expensive Italian designer bag.

7. The diamond brooch _____that he gave me_____ was a fake.

8. The book _____that I read_____ was unsuitable for the young children.

9. The seamstress _____who I hired_____ did not follow the pattern as directed.

10. I read an advertisement _____that I really liked_____.

Name _____ Clauses

Adjective Clauses

An **adjective clause** is a subordinate clause that modifies a noun or pronoun in the independent (or main) clause. The adjective clause is usually introduced by a relative pronoun such as *who, which,* or *that* and comes right after the word it modifies.

Example: The skirt <u>which is part of my school uniform</u> is blue and green plaid.

Underline the adjective clause once. Underline the relative pronoun twice. Write the word that it modifies in the blank.

man 1. The man <u>who</u> <u>sat at the next table in the restaurant</u> was smoking in the non-smoking section.

students 2. The students <u>who</u> <u>did not do their homework</u> got a detention.

bottle 3. I broke the crystal perfume bottle <u>that</u> <u>sat on my dresser</u>.

systems 4. The educational systems <u>that are currently in Europe, Asia, Africa, and South America</u> are quite dissimilar to those in North America.

civilization 5. The civilization <u>that</u> <u>spoke Latin</u> began to disappear after the collapse of the Roman Empire in 476 A.D.

languages 6. The modern languages <u>which</u> <u>eventually replaced Latin</u> include French, Spanish, Italian, Rumanian, and Portuguese.

contributions 7. Probably one of the most important contributions <u>that the Romans left behind</u> was their language.

pen 8. Did you take the black pen <u>that</u> <u>I was using</u>?

person 9. The person <u>who</u> <u>took my pen</u> got away with a very expensive writing instrument.

pen 10. It is the pen <u>that</u> <u>I got for a graduation present</u>.

Answer Key

Name _____   Clauses

Restrictive and Nonrestrictive Clauses

Adjective clauses can be restrictive or nonrestrictive. **Restrictive clauses** are essential to identifying a noun or pronoun, and they are not set apart by commas. **Nonrestrictive** clauses provide additional information about the noun or pronoun, but are not essential to specific identification. Nonrestrictive clauses are enclosed in commas.

Examples: The dress that Camilla wears to the theater is a simple black sheath. (restrictive)
Camilla's favorite dress, which she often wears to the theater, is a simple black sheath. (nonrestrictive)

Underline the adjective clause. Write RES if it is restrictive, and NRS if it is nonrestrictive. If there is no adjective clause, write NONE.

NRS 1. Baton Rouge, <u>which is the capital of Louisiana</u>, is in the heart of Cajun country.

NONE 2. When we are driving through Baton Rouge, we stop for delicious Cajun food.

RES 3. A city <u>which is noted for good Cajun food</u> is Baton Rouge.

NRS 4. Tricycles, <u>which are beginner bicycles</u>, have three wheels.

RES 5. Bicycles <u>that have three wheels</u> are called tricycles.

RES 6. The man <u>who is squinting</u> is the lifeguard.

NONE 7. Since the lifeguard has a large expanse of beach to watch, he must be very alert.

NRS 8. The lifeguard, <u>who happens to be my sister's boyfriend</u>, was late for duty.

NRS 9. Espresso, <u>which is my favorite drink</u>, is very strong.

RES 10. Coffee <u>that is grown in Colombia</u> tastes best to me.

© Carson Dellosa CD-3745   73

Name _____   Clauses

Adverb Clauses

An **adverb clause** is a subordinate clause that functions as an adverb to modify the independent clause. Adverb clauses answer the question *When, How, Where* and *Why*. They are introduced by a subordinating conjunction. Common subordinating conjunctions include *after, as, before, once, until, when, whenever, while, as if, as though, if, unless, whether, although, though, how, where, wherever, because, whereas,* and *since*.

Examples: <u>After we finish studying</u>, I'll order pizza. (when)
Alex answered the question <u>as if he were well-prepared</u>. (how)
<u>Wherever you go</u>, I'll find you. (where)
I failed <u>because I didn't study</u>. (why)

Underline the adverb clause in each sentence once. Underline the subordinating conjunction twice. Leave the sentence blank if there is no adverb clause.

1. The cookies taste great <u><u>because</u> they were made from scratch</u>.

2. <u><u>If</u> chicken is not properly washed</u>, harmful bacteria may be consumed.

3. <u><u>After</u> their first date</u>, Marcelo and Anna became good friends.

4. <u><u>Although</u> she worked almost every night</u>, Valerie was a full-time student.

5. Margaret read an interesting article <u><u>while</u> she sat on the bus</u>.

6. Mrs. Garland couldn't drive home <u><u>since</u> she lost her only key</u>.

7. I'll fix your glasses <u><u>while</u> you wait</u>.

8. <u><u>When</u> the daffodils bloom</u>, spring is here.

9. <u><u>Wherever</u> I go</u>, my little brother tags along.

10. <u><u>Although</u> alligators look very much like crocodiles</u>, they are usually not as dangerous.

© Carson Dellosa CD-3745   74

Name _____   Clauses

Adverb Clauses

An **adverb clause** is a subordinate clause that functions as an adverb to modify the independent clause. It is usually introduced by a subordinating conjunction.

Example: <u>Because the road had become so slick during the rainstorm</u>, Ms. Harris decided to postpone the field trip.

Complete each sentence below by adding an adverb clause.

1. _____When the mailman comes_____, all of the dogs in the neighborhood bark.

2. _____When the sun came up_____, I was surprised to see a barn owl.

3. _____Before we reached the hill top_____, we could see an eleventh century Rhine castle.

4. We spent the night in the German medieval town of Rothenburg der Tauber _____after we had dinner_____.

5. _____When I couldn't spell the word_____, we looked it up in the dictionary.

6. We were all skeptical, _____because Pam has played this trick before_____.

7. _____Because we are good friends_____, Jane bought her a pretty set of goblets.

8. _____Although she was careful_____, Jean almost got hit by the arrow.

9. Brandon could see the face of the clock in the darkness _____although the only light in the room was from the moon_____.

10. _____After looking for more than ten hours_____, Elizabeth found the water fountain too unsanitary to use.

© Carson Dellosa CD-3745   75

Name _____   Clauses

Noun Clauses

Subordinate clauses that function as nouns are called **noun clauses**. They can function in a sentence as a subject, direct object, predicate nominative, object of preposition, or anywhere that you find a simple noun.

Examples: <u>What he told me</u> was very cruel. (noun clause as subject)
I gave <u>whatever I could spare</u> to the homeless man. (noun clause as direct object)
Our study group will be <u>whoever shows up</u>. (noun clause as predicate nominative)
Mr. Phipps gives help after school to <u>whoever needs it</u>. (noun clause as object of the preposition)

Underline the noun clause in each sentence. Write its function: S for subject, DO for direct object, PN for predicate nominative, or OP for object of the preposition.

DO 1. Please tell me <u>who painted this landscape</u>.

PN 2. My concern is <u>that I won't have enough time</u>.

S 3. <u>Why you are dating him</u> is a mystery to me.

DO 4. He bought <u>what he needed at the sporting goods store</u>.

DO 5. I can't believe <u>what you did</u>.

OP 6. Betty talks to <u>whoever will listen</u>.

S 7. <u>Whoever is responsible for this</u> should step forward.

DO 8. The couch potatoes watched <u>whatever was on television</u>.

PN 9. The homecoming queen will be <u>whoever is most popular</u>.

S 10. <u>Whoever lives to the age of one hundred</u> is called a centenarian.

DO 11. You can do <u>whatever you want</u>.

OP 12. I will agree with <u>whatever you decide</u>.

© Carson Dellosa CD-3745   76

Answer Key

Name _____ **Clauses**

Review

Underline the clause in each sentence and decide which type of clause it is:

ADJ) Adjective Clause ADV) Adverb Clause
N) Noun Clause NONE) No subordinate Clause

N 1. In science class we learned that chalk is made of mostly calcium carbonate.

NONE 2. Advertisements encourage people to want products, and many people cannot distinguish between their wants and their needs.

ADJ 3. Liliuokani, who was the last queen of Hawaii, was an accomplished songwriter.

N 4. In accordance with school regulations, the school van may be driven by whomever is authorized by the principal.

ADV 5. When Pete lost his fortune, he found himself without friends.

NONE 6. Woodrow Wilson was a Virginian, a democrat, and the 28th President of the United States.

ADJ 7. The Indians who inhabited the area of Connecticut around the Naugatuck River were called the Perquots.

ADV 8. I wrote that poem when I was in a whimsical mood.

NONE 9. The beautiful day was rudely interrupted by a tornado.

ADJ 10. On the shelf are the three bisque dolls that I recently bought.

ADJ 11. Through their popular songs, Ella Fitzgerald, Lena Horne, and Leslie Uggams, who are all contemporary black vocalists, have enriched American music.

ADJ 12. The Great Wall of China, which is over 1500 miles long, was built to separate China from Mongolia.

© Carson Dellosa CD-3745 77

Name _____ **Phrases**

Identifying Phrases

Phrases are combinations of words that go together because they express a single idea. Unlike sentences and clauses, phrases do not contain both a subject and predicate.

Examples: The pretty, young woman caught his eye. (noun phrase)
I will be attending the coronation. (verb phrase)
He is married to a movie star. (prepositional phrase)

Look at each underlined phrase. Write in the blank if it is a noun phrase (NP), verb phrase (VP), adjective phrase (ADJP), adverb phrase (ADVP), or prepositional phrase (PP).

NP 1. Mary Beth was surprised when she couldn't get breakfast at Tiffany's.

VP 2. I am going on condition that my expenses are paid.

VP 3. The band that will be performing is an old favorite of mine.

ADJP 4. She caught a fish with blue gills.

PP 5. The seagulls soared over the dock.

NP 6. The mask with warts is really ugly.

NP 7. I was very amused by the pompous, old gentleman.

VP 8. He has been trying to meet the pretty tenant in 2C for months.

ADVP 9. The boss was thrilled at their work.

ADVP 10. The guests arrived late at night.

ADJP 11. The manager with the paychecks just left.

NP 12. The long, meandering path took all afternoon.

© Carson Dellosa CD-3745 78

Name _____ **Sentence Review**

Challenge

1. Determine the pattern in each sentence.
2. Identify the type of verbal or verbal phrase.
3. Determine if the verbal (or verbal phrase) is used as a noun (functioning as subject, direct object, predicate nominative, object of the preposition), an adjective, or adverb.

Pattern	Verbal	Function of Verbal
S-V	Gerund (Phrase)	Noun (S, DO, PN, OP)
S-V-DO	Participle (Phrase)	Adjective
S-V-DO-OC	Infinitive (Phrase)	Adverb
S-V-IO-DO		
S-LV-PN		
S-LV-PA		

1. To ride in a gondola is a thrill for children.

   Pattern: **S-LV-PN** Verbal: **infinitive** Function: **noun-S**

2. Singing to the tourists earned big tips for the gondola drivers.

   Pattern: **S-V-DO** Verbal: **gerund** Function: **noun-S**

3. Barbara wants to give her mother a book.

   Pattern: **S-V-DO** Verbal: **infinitive** Function: **noun-DO**

4. Following a crooked little street brought Barbara to a shop selling lovely Venetian glass.

   Pattern: **S-V-DO** Verbal: **gerund** Function: **noun-S**

5. She bought a necklace and matching bracelet from a famous Murano glass factory.

   Pattern: **S-V-DO** Verbal: **participle** Function: **adjective**

6. Barbara's favorite dish to eat in Venice is spaghetti with clams.

   Pattern: **S-LV-PN** Verbal: **infinitive** Function: **adjective**

© Carson Dellosa CD-3745 79

Name _____ **Sentence Review**

Challenge

1. Determine the sentence pattern of the independent clause in each sentence.
2. Identify the tense of the underlined verb.
3. Determine the type of subordinate clause.

Pattern	Tense		Clause
S-V	Simple Present	Present Progressive	Adjective
S-V-DO	Simple Past	Past Progressive	Adverb
S-V-DO-OC	Simple Future	Future Progressive	Noun
S-V-IO-DO	Present Perfect	Present Perfect Progressive.	
S-LV-PN	Past Perfect	Past Perfect Progressive.	
S-LV-PA	Future Perfect	Future Perfect Progressive.	

1. After settling in her hotel, Barbara will be heading for her favorite museum.

   Pattern: **S-V** Tense: **future prog.** Clause: **adverb**

2. This art museum, which is called the Galleria degli Uffizi, has been attracting millions of people from all over the world for many years.

   Pattern: **S-V-DO** Tense: **pres. perf. prog.** Clause: **adjective**

3. Barbara, who is an art history student, will spend several days in the Uffizi.

   Pattern: **S-V-DO** Tense: **future** Clause: **adjective**

4. As tourists were meandering through the halls of the Uffizi, Barbara was observing their reactions to different artists.

   Pattern: **S-V-DO** Tense: **past prog.** Clause: **adverb**

5. Whoever saw the paintings of Botticelli seemed mesmerized.

   Pattern: **S-LV-PA** Tense: **past** Clause: **noun**

6. Pallas and the Centaur, which was painted by Botticelli in 1485, was collecting a large crowd of admirers.

   Pattern: **S-V-DO** Tense: **past prog.** Clause: **adjective**

© Carson Dellosa CD-3745 80

Answer Key

Name _____ Sentence Review

Challenge

1. Determine the sentence structure in each sentence.
2. Look at the underlined noun and identify its function in the sentence.
3. Determine if the noun appears in an independent clause or subordinate clause.

Structure	Function	Clause
Simple (S)	Subject (Sub)	Independent (IND)
Compound (CD)	Direct Object (DO)	Subordinate (SUB)
Complex (CX)	Indirect Object (IO)	
Compound/Complex (CC)	Predicate Nominative (PN)	
	Object of the Preposition (OP)	

1. She particularly loves the Palatine Hill where the <u>ruins</u> of the palaces of Augustus, Nero, Caracalla, and Tiberius are located.

   Structure: __CX__ Function: __S__ Clause: __SUB__

2. Barbara walked from the Palantine Hills to the <u>valley</u> of the Roman Forum.

   Structure: __S__ Function: __OP__ Clause: __IND__

3. She observed the <u>Tempio di Vesta</u> where the goddess's flame was kept burning by the Vestal Virgins.

   Structure: __CX__ Function: __DO__ Clause: __IND__

4. The Arco di Tito at the end of the <u>expanse</u> of the forum was built in A.D. 81.

   Structure: __S__ Function: __OP__ Clause: __IND__

5. Barbara noted that the <u>atmosphere</u> of antiquity on the Palantine Hill enchanted Byron when he wrote *Childe Harold*.

   Structure: __CX__ Function: __S__ Clause: __SUB__

6. Another site that Barbara found intriguing was the Coliseum, and she spent hours at this place where Christians were literally thrown to the <u>lions</u>.

   Structure: __CC__ Function: __OP__ Clause: __SUB__

Name _____ Sentence Review

Challenge

Follow the directions given to create a sentence.

1. Write an S-V-DO sentence which has the participle form of the verb *to break* describing the direct object.

   We watched the breaking news.

2. Write an S-V-IO-DO sentence which uses the noun *gift* as the direct object.

   I gave Madeleine a gift.

3. Write a complex sentence containing the infinitive form of the verb *to discourage* as the subject of the main clause.

   To discourage class participation is something that a good teacher would never do.

4. Write a sentence using a direct quotation which contains the past perfect form of the verb *to run*.

   "Who had run in the marathon last year?" asked Joe.

5. Write a compound-complex sentence using the noun *book* as the object of a preposition in a subordinate clause.

   I'll buy it when I remember the name of the book.

Name _____ Sentence Review

Challenge

Follow the directions given to create a sentence.

1. Write an S-LV-PN sentence using an infinitive or infinitive phrase using the verb to miss.

   I am going to miss the bus.

2. Write a compound-complex sentence using the verb to run in the simple past tense in a subordinate clause.

   When Mrs. Miller ran for mayor, she was a retired teacher.

3. Write an S-LV-PA sentence which contains a demonstrative adjective to describe the subject.

   That girl is boisterous.

4. Write an S-V-DO sentence with a gerund or gerund phrase using the verb to read as the direct object.

   She loves to read.

5. Write a compound sentence in which the verb in both clauses is a future progressive form of the verb to go.

   I will be going to college in the fall, and my sister will be opening her new business.

Name _____ Sentence Combining

Sentence Combining

The following paragraph contains simple sentences with almost no variety in the sentence patterns. Rewrite the paragraph, making sure to include all information, but combining the sentences in ways that make the it more interesting and less choppy.

The Conciergerie is on the Cité in the heart of Paris. It includes three superb Gothic towers. The tour is of great historic interest. You enter through the Guardroom. It has stout pillars with carved capitals. The pillars support the Gothic vaulting. You then enter the Prisoner's Gallery. Here the prisoners had their hands roped behind their backs. Their collars were ripped wide open. Their hair was cut from the nape of their necks before walking into the clerk of court's yard. Next you see Marie Antoinette's prison. She existed in this cell from August 2, 1793 until October 16, 1793. Finally, you see a pathetic patch of grass and a tree. This is the Women's Courtyard. Twelve prisoners were selected daily for the guillotine. They said their farewells here.

The conciergerie on the Cité in the heart of Paris includes three superb Gothic Towers. The tour, which is of great historic interest, is entered through the Guardroom. Its stout pillars with carved capitals support the Gothic vaulting. You then enter the prisoner's Gallery where prisoners had their hands roped behind their backs, their collars ripped wide open, and their hair cut from the nape of their necks before walking into the clerk of court's yard. Next you see Marie Antoinette's prison cell where she existed from August 2, 1793 until October 13, 1793. Finally, you see a pathetic patch of grass and a tree called the Women's Courtyard. Twelve prisoners were selected daily for the guillotine and said their farewells here.

Answer Key

Name _____ Sentence Review

Sentence Combining

The following paragraph contains simple sentences with almost no variety in the sentence patterns. Rewrite the paragraph, making sure to include all information, but combining the sentences in ways that make the paragraph more interesting and less choppy.

La Boheme is one of the world's most beloved operas. It was written by Giacomo Puccini. It is based on a novel by Henri Murger. It is written in Italian. It was first performed in 1896 in Turin, Italy. It is set in the Latin Quarter of Paris. The time is about 1830. Act I opens in the attic studio of four struggling, but spirited young men. The male lead is Rudolpho. He is a writer. He meets a young seamstress named Mimi. They fall in love immediately. The lovers go through good times and hard times. Then Mimi becomes very ill. She leaves Rudolpho. In Act IV Mimi returns. She is dying. Rudolpho's friends try to help her. It is too late. Mimi has just come back to see Rudolpho once more. The opera ends with her death. Rudolpho anguishes in sadness and disbelief.

La Bohème, written by Giacoma Puccini, is one of the world's most beloved operas. Written in Italian, it is based on a novel by Henry Murger and first performed in 1896 in Turin, Italy. Act I, set in the Latin Quarter of Paris around 1830, opens in the attic studio of four struggling, but spirited young men. The male lead, Rudolpho, is a writer who meets a young seamstress named Mimi. They fall in love immediately and go through good times and hard times. Then Mimi becomes very ill and leaves Rudolpho. In Act IV the dying Mimi returns. Although Rudolpho's friends try to help her it is too late. Mimi has just come back to see Rudolpho once more, and the opera ends with Rudolpho anguishing in sadness and disbelief over her death.

Name _____ Sentence Review

Transformations

Read each sentence. Make all transformations requested.

Example: *The artist painted his mother a masterpiece.*

1. Change to a question in the present perfect tense.
   Has the artist painted a masterpiece?

1. We elected John class president.

   Change to a question in the future progressive tense.
   Will we be electing John class president?
   Change to passive voice in the simple past.
   John was elected class president by us.
   Change to S-V-O in the present perfect.
   John has been elected class president by us.

2. The shy girl became a bold leader.

   Change to a question in the simple future tense.
   Will the shy girl become a bold leader?
   Change to S-LV-PA in the present progressive tense.
   The shy girl is becoming a bold leader.

3. The directions are easy and the task is easy.

   Change to a negative statement in the present perfect tense.
   The directions have not been easy, and the task has not been easy.
   Change to a simple sentence with a compound subject.
   The directions and task are not easy.

Name _____ Sentence Review

Sentence Building

Write a sentence using the specific parts of speech requested in the exact order requested.

Example: noun + auxiliary + verb + preposition + article + adjective + noun. (7 words)
People are flocking to the new restaurant.

1. Demonstrative pronoun + linking verb + adjective + predicate adjective. (4 words)
   Those are ripe peaches.
2. Concrete noun + conjunction + concrete noun + verb + adverb. (5 words)
   Dogs and cats run quickly.
3. Collective noun + auxiliary verb + verb + preposition + adjective + noun. (6 words)
   People are voting for new roads.
4. Article + adjective + noun + adverb + verb + noun. (6 words)
   A brown bear suddenly attacked Mary.
5. Personal pronoun + linking verb + article + compound noun. (4 words)
   It is a notebook.
6. Indefinite pronoun + verb + infinitive. (4 words)
   Everyone likes to laugh.
7. Possessive noun + noun + adverb + verb. (4 words)
   Mary's friend quietly spoke.
8. Abstract noun + linking verb + article + adjective + abstract noun. (5 words)
   Love is a splendid thing.
9. Gerund + linking verb + article + adjective + noun. (5 words)
   Walking is a good exercise.
10. Participle + noun + linking verb + predicate adjective. (4 words)
    Twirling ballerinas are graceful.

Name _____ Word Usage

A lot and Allot

The phrase **a lot** means "to a considerable quantity or extent. " It is never spelled alot. The verb **allot** means "to give or assign." Don't confuse these spellings and meanings.

Example: He brought a lot of money.
Our club allots twenty percent of the proceeds from fundraising to local charities.

Use the correct form of *a lot* or *allot* in each sentence that follows.

1. Thanks ___a lot___ for your generous donation to our school fundraising effort.
2. We don't have ___a lot___ of money left after receiving that outrageous bill.
3. The Websters decided to ___allot___ $50.00 per paycheck to their vacation fund.
4. I have ___a lot___ of homework in math and social studies to do before bed.
5. Meghan ___allots___ a portion of her allowance each week to save for Christmas gifts for her family.
6. There was ___a lot___ of blaring music coming from the apartment above ours.
7. Marjorie knows ___a lot___ about caring for perennials, but she isn't as knowledgeable about annuals.
8. The school couldn't afford to ___allot___ money from the general fund to the new project.
9. Patrick thought that he had ___a lot___ of time to research the topic and write the essay.
10. The Browns ___allot___ ten percent of their income to church donations.

Answer Key

Name _____ Word Usage

Affect and Effect

Affect means "to act upon, assume, or influence" when used as a verb, and **effect** means "to produce or accomplish."

Example: Your study habits <u>affect</u> your grade. (influence)
Your good study habits should <u>effect</u> improvement in your grade. (produce)

Read each sentence carefully to determine if a form of *affect* or *effect* is needed. Write your answer on the line.

1. The movie last night ____affected____ me very much.

2. The book ____affected____ my thinking on the subject of weapons.

3. When she is with that crowd, Melissa ____affects____ an arrogant manner.

4. The board must ____effect____ immediate personnel cuts to avoid bankruptcy.

5. The threatening weather is ____affecting____ our outdoor plans.

6. The encounter group ____effected____ a definite change in attitudes among the participants.

7. Bringing computers into the classroom has ____effected____ better writing.

8. The teachers' in service ____effected____ an improved social studies curriculum.

9. Details of the candidate's private life ____affected____ his ratings in the polls.

10. The student's excuse did not ____affect____ the teacher's consequences.

11. The shoddy construction eventually ____effected____ an accident which resulted in a lawsuit.

12. Hurricane Camille ____affected____ the lives of thousands of people on the Gulf Coast.

© Carson Dellosa CD-3745   89

Name _____ Word Usage

As and Like

Like introduces a phrase and is a preposition. **As** and **as if** introduce clauses and are subordinating conjunctions. Although this distinction is often disregarded in informal speech, use *as* in formal, written language.

Examples: We need another dancer <u>like</u> him.
<u>As</u> I told you yesterday, you can't borrow the car.

Fill in the blanks with *like*, *as*, or *as if*.

1. It looks ____like____ rain today.

2. It looks ____as if____ it will rain today.

3. Damale, ____like____ her mother, is always late.

4. Your dog looks ____like____ a West Highland Terrier.

5. The student looked ____as if____ he could fall asleep any minute.

6. She sounds ____as if____ she is having an allergy attack.

7. ____Like____ my brother, I have red hair.

8. Your backpack looks ____like____ mine.

9. Rebecca handles a tennis racket ____like____ a pro.

10. My vision is not as sharp ____as____ your vision is.

11. Mallory looked ____as if____ she were ill.

12. He looked ____as if____ he were going to cry.

13. She walked ____as if____ she were in a trance.

14. The carousel looked ____like____ fun to the children.

15. The young child spoke ____like____ an adult.

© Carson Dellosa CD-3745   90

Name _____ Word Usage

Between and Among

Between is used to describe the relationship of a person or thing to one other person or thing. Between can also refer to more than two persons or things when each person or object is considered in its relationship to others. **Among** is generally used when three or more persons or things are involved.

Examples: We divided the treats <u>between</u> Alex and Alyssa.
Cooperation <u>between</u> workers is essential in the workplace.
We divided the treats <u>among</u> the five children.

Read each sentence and write *between* or *among* as appropriate.

1. I see no difference in the quality ____between____ these two brands.

2. We need to choose soon from ____among____ all the applicants.

3. I'm sure that ____among____ the many choices at the pound, this dog is the perfect one for Nancy.

4. Let's keep that information ____between____ you and me.

5. There was a lot of tension ____between____ Marie and the other girls in the class.

6. We found the remote lodged ____between____ the two cushions.

7. It was hard to choose ____among____ the candidates because we didn't like any of them.

8. Walking through the forest, we saw a few sycamores ____among____ the elms.

9. ____Among____ the many intriguing cookbooks on the bookstore shelf was a particularly intriguing one from Tuscany.

10. The treasures of the Uffizzi Museum in Florence are ____among____ the most beautiful pieces of art in the world.

11. The couple couldn't decide ____among____ Rome, Paris, or London for their honeymoon.

© Carson Dellosa CD-3745   91

Name _____ Word Usage

Lie and Lay

The verb **lie** means "to recline" and is intransitive (does not require a direct object). The verb **lay** means "put" and is transitive (requires a direct object) or must be in the passive voice. The principal parts of the verb are as follows:

basic form	past tense	past participle
lie	lay	lain
lay	laid	laid

Examples: She will <u>lie</u> in bed most of the morning. (basic form of lie in future tense)
After the long jog, I <u>lay</u> on the sofa for twenty minutes. (past tense of lie)
This memo has <u>lain</u> on the desk all day. (Past participle form of lie)
Please <u>lay</u> that crate on the floor. (basic form of lay in the present tense)
He <u>laid</u> the crate on the floor with a clatter. (past tense of lay)
He had <u>laid</u> the blame on me at that time. (past participle form of lay)
The book was <u>laid</u> on the shelf. (past form of lay in the passive voice)

Fill in the blank with the correct form of *lie* or *lay*.

1. The mountains ____lay____ before us when we discovered car trouble.

2. The phone message has ____lain____ unreturned for days.

3. I had ____laid____ two dollars on the counter.

4. I like to ____lie____ on my back in the sun for about twenty minutes.

5. Your bicycle has ____lain____ on the sidewalk too long.

6. Chip ____laid____ his books next to his locker.

7. How long has he ____lain____ there?

8. I am going to ____lie____ down.

9. ____Lay____ the keys where I can see them.

10. ____Lie____ down on the bed if you are tired.

11. I have ____laid____ the papers somewhere and now I can't find them!

© Carson Dellosa CD-3745   92

Answer Key

Name _____ Word Usage

Sit and Set

Sit means "to place oneself" and is an intransitive verb that does not require an object.
Set means "to put" or "to place" and is a transitive verb, and requires an object or use in passive construction.

Example: Don't sit on the sofa in those sweaty clothes.
            I set the remote on the coffee table.
            The date was set last fall. (passive)

Exceptions: The sun set.
            They set out at dawn.
            Wait a few hours for the paint to set.

Fill in the blank with the correct form of _sit_ or _set_.

1. _____Set_____ your purse on the counter and come here.

2. I will _____set_____ my alarm for four in the morning.

3. I will _____sit_____ next to Kali at the movies.

4. We had been _____sitting_____ at the gate for two hours before the flight was cancelled.

5. I will be _____sitting_____ in the center balcony during the performance.

6. The crew _____set_____ the stage as quickly as they could.

7. Don't _____set_____ the clock until you check with the station.

8. I _____set_____ my suitcase on the conveyor belt.

9. Mildred _____set_____ the mail on my desk.

10. The company's sales _____set_____ a record last week.

11. All we could do was _____sit_____ and wait.

12. Never _____sit_____ in Papa Bear's chair.

© Carson Dellosa CD-3745   93

Name _____ Punctuation

Commas

Comma Usage does vary, but the following rules should be helpful:
1. Use a comma to separate independent clauses joined by the coordinating conjunctions _and, but, yet, neither, nor, or, so_ or _yet_, unless each clause is very short.

Examples: Brad will bring a variety of snacks, and Sarah will bring three or four videos.
           The sky darkened, and the rain fell. (two short independent clauses)

2. Use a comma to separate a dependent (subordinate) clause from the main clause when the subordinate clause comes first. When the subordinate clause is in the middle, set it off with commas only if it is not essential to identifying the noun that precedes it.

Examples: The city in Louisiana which is the capital is Baton Rouge. (essential)
           Baton Rouge, which is the capital of Louisiana, is in Cajun country.
           (not essential)

Place commas where appropriate in each sentence. Some sentences need no commas.

1. The chapter, which comes next, contains the scary part.

2. Chapter 24, which contains the scary part, was assigned for homework.

3. Although they aren't millionaires, they travel in style.

4. The room was tiny, and the view was not so good.

5. The bed in the room was lumpy, but she fell asleep anyway.

6. She must set the alarm or risk missing the train.

7. If she missed the train, she would be late for a very important appointment.

8. Alex missed the ticketing deadline, so his ticket was much more expensive.

9. When you read her resumé, you'll see that she is well-qualified.

10. The man whom they met in Paris was from Afghanistan.

© Carson Dellosa CD-3745   94

Name _____ Punctuation

Commas

Here are more uses for commas:
1. Use the **comma** to separate words, phrases, and clauses in a series.

Example: Stop, look, and listen.

2. Use a comma to separate two or more adjectives when they modify the same noun. _And, or,_ or _nor_ make commas unnecessary when they are placed between adjectives. If an adjective actually modifies the adjective that follows it as well as the noun, do not separate the adjectives with a comma.

Examples: Sherry was a loquacious, gregarious person. (modify same noun)
           Sherry was loquacious and gregarious. (uses and between adjectives)
           The garden was surrounded by an old stone fence. (1st adjective modifies 2nd adjective)

Add commas where they are appropriate. Some sentences do not need commas.

1. She has midterm exams this week in English, Social Studies, and Biology.

2. Do you need to change the size or style of the lettering?

3. The home is spacious and comfortable.

4. The speaker was nervous, sweating, and miserable.

5. The well-stocked grocery store contains anything you might need.

6. He was a cunning military analyst.

7. Trains in Germany are usually fast, efficient, comfortable, and plentiful.

8. Pascali, Pristine, Fragrant, Cloud, and Brandy are some of my favorite roses.

9. Nathan dated Natalie, Nicole, Natasha, Nancy, Nina, and Nadine in the same year.

10. Pecans, chocolate chips, butter, sugar, eggs, and flour are in these cookies.

11. Eat, drink, and be merry!

12. Her campaign for governor was aggressive, hard-hitting, and expensive.

© Carson Dellosa CD-3745   95

Name _____ Punctuation

Colons

1. A colon can signal a reader's expectations about the text that follows:
   Example: Only one choice remained: do it myself.
2. A colon is used to introduce lists of words, phrases, and even clauses:
   Examples: There are three ingredients left to include: basil, cream, and salt.
              Candice's home is large: four bedrooms, three baths, a gameroom,
              computer room, and workout room.
              These steps are important before traveling abroad: get a passport, check to
              see if a visa is required, and exchange some currency in advance.
3. The colon is not used to introduce lists if the list is the object of the preposition, or object of the verb.
   Example: Sam went shopping for jeans, sweaters, and socks.

Add a colon in the appropriate place in each sentence. Do nothing if no colon is needed.

1. A good vinaigrette needs these ingredients: extra virgin olive oil, wine vinegar, Dijon mustard, and garlic.

2. John attributed his undeserved perfect score on the quiz to one thing: luck.

3. Allen got a sprained ankle, sunburn, splinters, and an allergy attack during the hike.

4. Caution: The undertow is strong.

5. The following teachers will be attending a conference today: Ms. Pendleton, Mr. Rosinia, and Mrs. West.

6. Notice Drafts will count as 20% of your total score.

7. I am changing planes in Dallas, Salt Lake City, and Portland.

8. Two tasks remained before Janice could go to the movie: complete her homework, and wash the dog.

9. His upcoming blind date was intriguing: a former homecoming queen, class valedictorian, and a Karate blackbelt.

10. James will be applying to Princeton, University of Virginia, and Harvard.

© Carson Dellosa CD-3745   96

Answer Key

Colons

The following special situations use colons:
1. Business letter salutations   *Dear Mr. Allen:*
2. Title and subtitle   *Reading in the 90's: Improving Comprehension*
3. Hours and minutes   *12:02 p.m.*
4. Acts and scenes of play   *Hamlet, II:1*
5. Publisher's location and name   *New York: McGraw-Hill*

Rewrite each of the following using a colon.

1. six o'clock

   6:00

2. Shakespeare (title) The Complete Works (subtitle)

   Shakespeare: The Complete Works

3. The American Publishing Company in Hartford

   Hartford: The American Publishing Company

4. page 6 in volume 2 of The History of the New World

   The History of the New World, Volume 2: page 6

5. Louisiana (title) The Land and Its People (subtitle)

   Louisiana: The Land and Its People

6. Scene 2 in Act I of She Stoops to Conquer

   She Stoops to Conquer, II: I

7. Dear Sir

   Dear Sir:

8. Rand McNally and Co. in Chicago

   Chicago: Rand McNally and Co.

9. scene 3 in Act III of Our Town

   Our Town, III: 3

10. ten o'clock

    10:00

Quotation Marks

Quotation marks enclose the words used by a speaker or writer. Periods and commas go inside the closing quotation mark in the preferred American style, (although you may also see the British style which can vary). Question marks and exclamation points go inside the closing quotation marks when they apply only to the quoted words. Indirect quotations do not use quotation marks.

Examples: "Come here," said Marie. (inside comma)
Marie said, "Come here." (inside period)
"Won't you come?" asked Marie. (question mark inside)
Did you hear Marie ask, "Won't you come"? (question mark outside)
Marie asked that I come. (indirect quotation)

Rewrite each sentence with quotation marks and appropriate placement of end punctuation.

1. Look out yelled Pete.

   "Look out!" yelled Pete.

2. Stop saying Look out!

   "Stop saying, 'Look out!'"

3. The cashier said You need to have correct change.

   The cashier said, "You need to have correct change."

4. Do you know what time registration begins asked Laura.

   Do you know what time registration begins?" asked Laura.

5. Did I actually hear her ask Who wants to skip class?

   "Did I actually hear her ask, 'Who wants to skip class?'"

6. Let's eat anchovy pizza tonight suggested Melanie.

   "Let's eat anchovy pizza tonight," suggested Melanie.

7. Alvin countered Let's either have Mexican food or a vegetarian meal.

   Alvin countered, "Let's either have Mexican food or a vegetarian meal."

noun
1

pronoun
2

verb
3

adjective
4

© CD-3745

adverb
5

preposition
6

conjunction
7

interjection
8

© CD-3745

simple past
9

simple present
10

simple future
11

past perfect
12

© CD-3745

present perfect
13

future perfect
14

She had gone to the game to watch her cousin play.
15

That old picture is important to my mother.
16

© CD-3745

Ryan <u>smiles</u> more than anyone I know.

17

Fred <u>had used</u> that excuse before.

18

I <u>will have gotten</u> enough votes by that time.

19

Mike <u>has apologized</u> to the class.

20

The party <u>was held</u> in the spring.

21

The children <u>built</u> the snowman on the hill.

22

The lecture <u>will have begun</u> before we arrive at the arena.

23

The money <u>has been donated</u> to a worthy cause.

24

Jim <u>had</u> a great parking space near the door.

25

The pilot <u>will have flown</u> seven missions by next month.

26

I <u>will create</u> a beautiful scenery for the play.

27

The girl in the hat <u>has been</u> on the bench for an hour.

28

He had <u>listened</u> to that story before.

29

The woman <u>rejoiced</u> at the good news.

30

The vampire <u>will arise</u> after the sun sets.

31

They <u>will have run</u> fourteen miles by tonight.

32

33 The cat has eaten, Chris.

34 I had washed the car already.

35 Winnie had watched the whole movie last night.

36 Hal did his homework in class.

37 The painter will finish the job soon.

38 Glenda had slipped on the ice before it melted.

39 I have done all my chores.

40 simple subject

41 simple predicate

42 complete subject

43 complete predicate

44 compound simple subject

45 compound simple predicate

46 compound complete subject

47 compound complete predicate

48 simple subject and complete predicate

complete subject and simple predicate 49	**compound subject and simple predicate** 50	**complete subject and complete predicate** 51	**simple subject and compound complete predicate** 52
compound simple subject and compound simple predicate 53	**compound complete subject and compound complete predicate** 54	**S-V** 55	**S-V-O** 56
S-V-IO-DO 57	**S-LV-PN** 58	**S-LV-PA** 59	subject / predicate 60
verb ... and ... verb 61	subject ... verb / verb 62	subject verb / direct object 63	subject verb / direct object / indirect object 64

© CD-3745 (on each card)

65 — subject | linking verb \ predicate adjective
© CD-3745

66 — subject | linking verb \ predicate nominative
© CD-3745

67 — verb \ adverb
© CD-3745

68 — verb \ adverb \ adverb
© CD-3745

69 — noun | adjective \ adverb
© CD-3745

70 — noun | prep. \ object of preposition
© CD-3745

72 — verb | prep. \ object of preposition
© CD-3745

72 — The sun rises in the east.
© CD-3745

73 — The odd man carried the paper bag.
© CD-3745

74 — Lou's essay is the winner of the contest.
© CD-3745

75 — Mrs. Coate gave James a gentle nudge.
© CD-3745

76 — The old flower turned brown.
© CD-3745

77 — The candy tasted rather tart.
© CD-3745

78 — Vic and Betty ride bicycles in the park.
© CD-3745

79 — Jason will run for class president and might win.
© CD-3745

80 — We devoured the entire meal in fifteen minutes!
© CD-3745

We saw a green snake under the porch yesterday.

© CD-3745   81

independent clause

© CD-3745   82

dependent clause

© CD-3745   83

she ran the mile in three minutes

© CD-3745   84

she would rather work in the hospital

© CD-3745   85

beneath the chair and next to the window

© CD-3745   86

they golf every Wednesday

© CD-3745   87

who sat on the fresh paint

© CD-3745   88

up the stairs and down the hall

© CD-3745   89

the police officer's directions were excellent

© CD-3745   90

the color of the sweater made a big difference

© CD-3745   91

after I walked through the doors of the building

© CD-3745   92

the woman leaves for Wyoming after class today

© CD-3745   93

we spent the morning on the bus

© CD-3745   94

after he finished the last drop of water

© CD-3745   95

the jacket was found in the back seat

© CD-3745   96